faiThGirLz!™

NO BOYS allowed

Devotions for Girls

Written by Kristi Holl
with Jennifer Vogtlin

*Calvary at
Village Green*

Zonder**kidz**

Zonderkidz®

The children's group of Zondervan

www.zonderkidz.com

No Boys Allowed
Text copyright © 2004 by Michelle Medlock Adams

Requests for information should be addressed to:
Zonderkidz, 5300 Patterson Ave. SE, Grand Rapids, Michigan 49530

ISBN: 0-310-70718-8

Zonderkidz is a trademark of Zondervan

Interior design: Susan Ambs
Art direction: Michelle Lenger

Printed in the United States

04 05 06 07 /❖DC/ 10 9 8 7 6 5 4 3 2 1

Contents

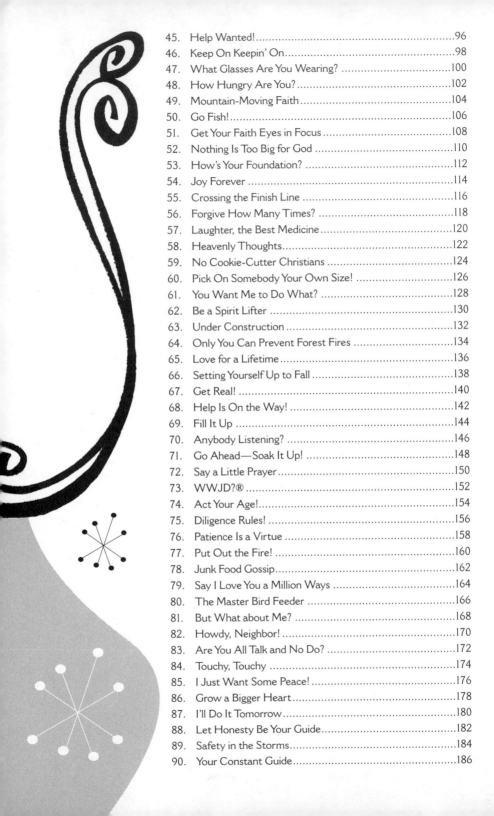

So we fix our eyes not on what is seen, but on what is unseen.
For what is seen is temporary, but what is unseen is eternal.
— *2 Corinthians 4:18*

Devotion #1

"A heart at peace gives life to the body, but
envy rots the bones."—Proverbs 14:30 (NIV)

The Green-Eyed Monster

A peaceful heart is relaxed and easy, not tense
and fearful. This peace of mind and heart will
actually give you a longer, healthier life. But envy and
jealousy gnaw at you, deep inside. The Bible says it can
even rot your bones. That's pretty unhealthy!

Envy and jealousy can take you totally by surprise. You
see your dad holding your little step-sister or hugging his new
wife. The stab of jealousy can jab hard. Or maybe it's a milder
form of envy. You'd give anything for your classmate's designer
jeans. Instead, you wear big sister's hand-me-downs and
shop at thrift stores.

These are perfectly innocent moments, but how you
feel during these times—and what you do about it—
is what counts.

Jealousy is sneaky. It's natural to compare
ourselves to others or want what someone else has. But when that comparison
makes us unhappy, we're probably feeling jealous. Notice how you feel about
the good fortune of others: their cool
clothes, perfect looks, or their attention in
the spotlight. If you feel anything but peace

in your heart, you might be feeling jealous. Can you be happy for them instead? Can you compliment them on an outstanding performance or their pretty outfit? Taking positive action is a quick way to kill that green-eyed monster.

The Bible says in James 3:16 that where you have envy (which is another word for jealousy), you will find disorder and every evil practice. Not good! The sooner you tackle these emotions, the easier they are to defeat. God wants you to have a heart filled with peace. A heart at peace is a heart focused on God. So the next time you feel jealous, ask God to help you put jealousy in its place—out of your life!

Did You Know

... you can read about jealousy in Genesis 37? When Joseph's half-brothers envied his fancy clothes and were jealous of Joseph's special attention, their evil actions changed history!

More To Explore: Read James 3:13–18

GirL TaLk:

Are you jealous of someone? Be honest with yourself, but more importantly, be honest with God. He will help you overcome jealousy.

God TaLk:

Lord, I am really jealous of _____. I know that I shouldn't be, but I am. Forgive me. Please help me to love this person like you do. Thank you for all the good things in my life. Help me to focus on all the blessings I already have instead of envying the blessings of others. And thank you for blessing _____. I know you have more than enough blessings to go around. Amen.

Devotion #2

"What is the price of five sparrows? A couple of pennies? Yet God does not forget a single one of them. And the very hairs on your head are all numbered. So don't be afraid; you are more valuable to him than a whole flock of sparrows."—Luke 12:6–7 (NLT)

MiLLioN DoLLar Hair

If God cares for small birds that are worth only a couple pennies, then imagine how much more he cares for you. He watches over you so closely that he even knows how many hairs you have on your head. You don't ever need to be afraid. God says you are *valuable*: of great worth, precious, and priceless!

Get outside for a minute. Watch the birds overhead as they glide on the breeze without a care in the world. They aren't worried about where their next worm is coming from! "Look at the birds. They don't need to plant or harvest or put food in barns because your heavenly Father feeds them. And you are far more valuable to him than they are." (Matthew 6:26 NLT) If God provides every need for the birds, how much more will he take care of you?

Thinking deeply about this truth can help when you feel sad and lonely, when you think no one notices you. If he is concerned enough to count every hair on your head, then God is even more concerned about your nightmares, that fight with your friend, your dream of being a nurse, and yes, even your frizzy hair. God—the Creator of the whole universe—cares deeply and personally about *you*.

You are precious to God!

Did You Know

. . . that even David, great king of Israel and close friend to God, felt unimportant and overlooked at times? Read Psalm 13.

God Talk:

"Lord, I'm feeling all alone today. I don't know why I'm so valuable to you, but I thank you for your unfailing love. Please help me remember how much you care for me. Amen."

More To Explore: Luke 12:22–31

Girl Talk:

Have you ever felt lonely, even if you're around by family or friends? Take a walk in a park, or look through a nature magazine, to remind you that God takes care of everything in this world, including you! It's a perfect time to ask God to fill you with his love.

Fun Factoid:

An average head has approximately 100,000 hairs on it. Redheads have about 90,000 hairs. Brunettes have about 110,000 hairs, and blondes have about 140,000 hairs.

Devotion #3

"A troublemaker plants seeds of strife;
gossip separates the best of friends."
—Proverbs 16:28 (NLT)

Tame The Tongue

We all know people who enjoy stirring up trouble by telling people's secrets. Although it's tempting to do this, beware! It can cause a permanent division between even the best of best friends.

You know how it is. Someone whispers that they know Trish's boyfriend is IMing another girl. Or Ms. Gossip tells a juicy tidbit about Alyssa's "F" on the science test. Or maybe you spent the night at your friend's house and overheard a nasty fight between your friend's parents. You're so tempted to repeat it when you're asked how you enjoyed your sleepover. It's especially hard not to gossip about a friend when she's hurt your feelings. We want to tell someone! Do you want to be known as a troublemaker? No! Gossip hurts others, and it can come back to hurt you too when you lose friends. What's a better choice? "He who covers and forgives an offense seeks love, but he who repeats or harps on a matter separates even close friends." (Proverbs 17:9 NIV)

Instead of repeating someone's private information, zip your lip and sit on it. If you've already gossiped, ask God's forgiveness. Then go back to those you spread tales to and admit you were wrong to gossip. Last, apologize to your friend for repeating a story about her. Next time you're tempted to gossip, "cover and forgive an offense" and keep your friendship close and loving.

Avoid being a troublemaker who stirs up conflict. Instead, control your tongue and tell any "secrets" you know about others only to God. Then pray for that person, like a *real* friend would.

Did You Know

. . . that James, brother of Jesus and author of the book of James, says the tongue is "full of wickedness, and poisons every part of the body"? (James 3:6 LB) Makes you think, doesn't it?

More To Explore: Psalm 34:13–14; Proverbs 15:4

Girl Talk:

Have you caused strife through gossip lately? What should you do when someone wants to share gossip with you?

God Talk:

"Father, I sometimes tell secrets or repeat information that I shouldn't. I realize this is wrong, and I want to do better. I ask that you keep my mouth in line and my heart pure. Help me to be a trustworthy friend. I want my tongue to praise, not hurt. Thank you. Amen."

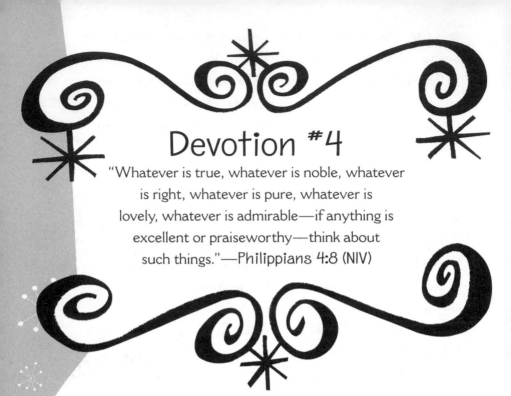

Devotion #4

"Whatever is true, whatever is noble, whatever is right, whatever is pure, whatever is lovely, whatever is admirable—if anything is excellent or praiseworthy—think about such things."—Philippians 4:8 (NIV)

Whatever!

Your mind is the control center for your whole body, so feed it great food! What makes a great "mind meal"? Think about what is real and true and worth depending on. Think about people with high moral qualities who deserve honor. Focus on things that are free from error—like God's Word. No matter who or what you think about, concentrate on the things of highest quality.

We make choices every day. Should we watch that video with our friends, even though the language and morals are bad? What about the books and magazines you choose, or the music you listen to? Are you feeding your mind with excellent images and words? If not, choose a video that is high quality in language and behavior, one that leaves you with peace of mind instead of feelings of guilt. Read stories of admirable heroes, those who make a positive difference in the world. Listen to music you like, but be sure the songs' words are praiseworthy.

Thinking great thoughts also helps us control our feelings. Look hard for something good in a bad situation, and think about that instead. Maybe your friend canceled your shopping trip, but now you have time to read that great book. Maybe in gym you got paired with the new girl instead of your best friend, so choose to be glad for a chance to make a new friend. *Your thoughts control your feelings*.

Did You Know

. . . that Solomon, the wisest man who ever lived, let his thoughts lead him astray? Read 1 Kings 11:1–14 to learn more.

God Talk:

"Lord, I thank you for giving me choice in what I do. Please help me to make the right choices, to do what is pure and excellent. I want to grow closer to you through the choices I make. Amen."

More To Explore: Proverbs 23:7, Matthew 5:6–9

Girl Talk:

If you think mean thoughts, how do you feel? If you forgive someone, how does that make you feel? Which one feels better?

Devotion #5

"Obscene stories, foolish talk, and coarse jokes—
these are not for you. Instead, let there be
thankfulness to God."—
Ephesians 5:4 (NLT)

Phew! Got Mouthwash?

Your beautiful voice was not created for telling
foul jokes and stories, nor for conversation that lacks
good sense or judgment. Instead, in your conversations,
focus on the good things in your life. Remind each other of
God's blessings and be thankful.

Have you ever sat at the lunch table at school, trapped
between two people telling dirty jokes or making indecent
comments? Maybe it happened to you at someone's sleepover,
at the mall, or in the theater waiting for a movie to start.
Wanting badly to fit in, some girls are tempted to join the
foolish talk or laugh at the dirty stories. Others
choose to say nothing. Not cool either. Being
quiet and just listening while others use foul
talk is not what God wants for you.

What can you do in such situations?
Be gutsy. Speak up against the foul talk.
Others may be uncomfortable with it as
well, and they'll be glad you said something. If the coarse jokes continue, then

avoid these people. They are not the kind of friends God wants for you.

Do you have trouble turning aside from off-color stories and talk? If talking this way is a real temptation for you, perhaps you have a "heart condition" and need a check-up. "For out of the overflow of the heart the mouth speaks." (Matthew 12:34 NIV)

Fill your heart with good, positive thoughts from God's Word, for this will determine your words. Then remind your friends of all that God has done, and be thankful.

Did You Know

. . . the book of Proverbs was written to give "knowledge and discretion (good judgment) to the young"? (Proverbs 1:4, NIV) Proverbs was written for you, so get to know it well!

More To Explore: Proverbs 4:23–27

Girl Talk:

Have you told dirty jokes or stories to fit in? Think back to a time where you made the wrong choice. Ask God to forgive you, and ask forgiveness from any person involved.

God Talk:

"Father, it is so hard to keep a pure mind and heart. I want to stand up for you, but my courage fails me. Please help me speak up against filthy talk, and help me guard against it in my heart. Thank you. Amen."

Fun Factoid:

A good clean laugh beats gossip any day! Doctors call laughter "inner jogging" because it gives the muscles of your face, shoulders, diaphragm, and abdomen a good workout!

17

Devotion #6

"Aim for perfection, listen to my appeal, be of one mind, live in peace. And the God of love and peace will be with you."
—2 Corinthians 13:11 (NIV)

Living in Peace

Paul says we should make perfection our goal, especially in our relationships, with friends, teachers, and family members. Learn to live peaceably and agree with one another. The more you try to do this, the more you will experience God's love and peace in your life.

Do you ever aim for perfection? Do you try to achieve a perfect math score? Do you attempt the perfect batch of chocolate chip cookies or the perfect swan dive? Do you look for the perfect hair cut and clothes for a party? We aim for perfection—for excellence—many times in our lives. As we keep trying, we keep improving and getting closer to our goals. But only God is actually perfect, or ever will be. He is happy with us if we keep growing and trying to do better. It's like shooting a bow and arrow. You're aiming for a perfect bull's-eye, but you're pleased as your arrows get closer and closer.

Even more important than tests and sports and clothes is how we live with people. Will we ever live perfectly with our friends and family members? No, but we can head in that direction. Don't dish out that put-down you usually snap at your brother. Don't bicker about whose turn it is to empty the dishwasher or fold laundry. Don't be touchy when your best friend doesn't give you her undivided attention at the ball game.

Can't do this on your own? No problem! God is the source of the love and peace you need, and he wants to help you live in harmony with others. Just ask him to help you. And your reward? The God of love and peace will be with you. How terrific is that!

Did You Know

. . . that it's God who gives you the desire to get along and then the power to carry it out? Read Philippians 2:13.

God Talk:

"Lord, I know I have a hard time getting along with my family and friends sometimes. Please help me to help others willingly and with joy. Thank you for the peace you bring to my life. Amen."

More To Explore: Romans 12:14–18

Girl Talk:

In the past day or so, have you helped at home with a loving heart or a resentful attitude? Could you do better next time?

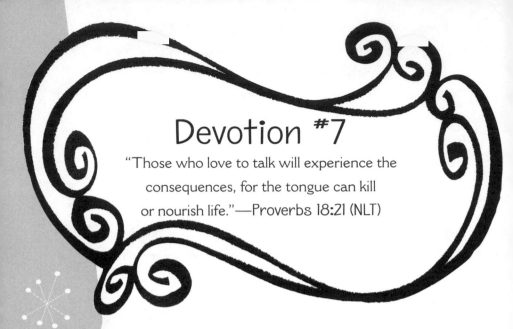

Devotion #7

"Those who love to talk will experience the consequences, for the tongue can kill or nourish life."—Proverbs 18:21 (NLT)

Power-Packed Words

Talk about powerful words! But whose tongue has the power of life and death in it? Believe it or not, *yours*. Do you love to talk? Then beware. The words you speak can nourish yourself and bring others joy. Or your words can bring death: dead friendships, dead hopes, and dead opportunities. It's your choice.

Nothing's more fun than a gab session after school over a soda, or on the phone late at night. Let's face it. Girls love to talk. A lot! There's nothing wrong with that, but pay attention to what you say. If your friend tells you about her science fair idea, you can say, "Fabulous idea. How'd you ever think of something that cool?" Or you can say, "At least ten people in class will do that project. It's soooo lame." Guess which words bring life and joy to your friend, and which ones kill her idea?

Before speaking, pause a moment and consider the effect of your words. How do you think the person receiving them will feel? Sometimes we get so busy sounding clever and making snappy wisecracks that we forget the pain our remarks can cause someone else. And there are consequences for that. Friendships don't last long when you dish out a steady diet of negative comments, criticism, and (not so funny) put-downs. Opportunities for jobs and fun also go to someone else—a girl with a more positive mouth.

Use your words to nurture the people in your life. Be uplifting and spread a little joy around. Then sit back and watch it all come back to you, many times over!

Did You Know

. . . the NIV translation of the Bible mentions the word "tongue" 61 times? God must think what you say is very important!

More To Explore:

Proverbs 10:19–21 and Ecclesiastes 10:12–14

Girl Talk:

Do you use your words as weapons, or do you use your words to uplift others?

God Talk:

"Lord, I realize that all words have power. I want my words to have a positive effect and lift up others. Help me to choose my words wisely. Amen."

Beauty 101:

As you work on what comes out of your mouth, don't forget the lips themselves! You can never go wrong with using lip gloss, in either clear or soft berry shades.

Devotion #8

"Truthful lips endure forever, but a lying tongue lasts only a moment." —Proverbs 12:19 (NIV)

True or False?

Truth will stand the test of time, while lies are soon exposed for what they are. Someone who lies may be believed for a short while, but the truth has a way of coming out.

Nobody likes to be lied about. It hurts—a lot! Maybe you overhear your friend say you got your new skirt at Goodwill, when she knows it was a gift from your favorite aunt. Or a jealous girl tells others that you cheated to get that "A" on your English test, when you studied hard for three solid hours for that grade. What do you do?

Do speak up—calmly—and tell the truth of the matter. It's fine to correct the lie with the truth. But keep it short and simple, then drop it or change the subject. Don't gossip or run the other person down, no matter how tempting the idea is. We don't like to admit it sometimes, but we want the other person to hurt as badly as we do, or be just as embarrassed. They deserve it, right? Maybe, but resist that temptation. Simply tell the truth, then change the subject. Someone's lie may be believed for a short while, but in time (often by your pure speech and behavior), the lies will be shown for what they are.

Proverbs 12:17 says "a good man is known by his truthfulness; a false man by deceit and lies." Determine to be a girl known for telling the truth—make that your reputation—and your words will stand the test of time.

Did You Know

. . . a witness in a trial who tells information they know to be false can be put in jail? Telling the truth is important, everywhere you go!

More To Explore: Acts 5

Girl Talk:

Do you think little white lies are OK? If so, when does a white lie become a beige lie and a gray lie and then a full-blown black lie?

God Talk:

"Lord, it is really tough to be truthful all the time, but I want to be. Please help me tell the truth—at all times—in every situation. Amen."

Fun Factoid:

According to a recent study, most people lie. In fact, most will tell an average of two to three lies during a ten-minute conversation!

Devotion #9

"My kinsmen have gone away; my friends have forgotten me." —Job 19:14 (NIV)

Help! Where Did Everybody Go?

It's a sad time when we feel our relatives have failed us and gone away, or our friends have turned against us. We may feel forgotten, as if we've been dismissed from their minds. At times we may even wonder if they remember we exist.

Has your best friend been spending her time lately with the new girl in school? Has she forgotten that you're the one she is supposed to call on the phone at night, or Instant Message, or take to the movies? Maybe it's even worse. Your dad or mom has left, and weeks go by without a phone call or letter or e-mail. How could they have gone away like that?

First, check the truth behind your feelings. We can *feel* abandoned when we're not being rejected at all. Has your best friend really turned against you? Check out the facts. She may have simply been extra busy at home. If you find she has indeed turned against you, ask why. If you've done something to hurt or offend her, apologize and heal the friendship. But if, for reasons of her own choosing, she has broken off the friendship, it will hurt until you make new friends to fill the gap. And you'll feel the ache until you can be with Mom or Dad again. Those feelings are perfectly normal.

Always remember something important at times like these. "Even if my father and mother abandon me, the Lord will hold me close." On those days when friends and family fail you, God will never leave you. Go to him in prayer. He always welcomes you with open arms!

Did You Know

. . . other Faithgirlz go through this very conflict? Sophie watches Fiona hang out with Julia and her friends in *Sophie's World*. Maggie also feels dumped in this book.

More To Explore: Proverbs 17:9

Girl Talk:

Has your best friend ever ignored you? Has she become better friends with someone else? How does that make you feel?

God Talk:

"Lord, help me to be a good friend. Help me to be the kind of friend that you have always been to me. Please help me to lean on you for love and friendship. I love you. Amen."

Fun Factoid:

Statistics show that an average person will make about 150 real friends and more than 2,000 acquaintances in a lifetime.

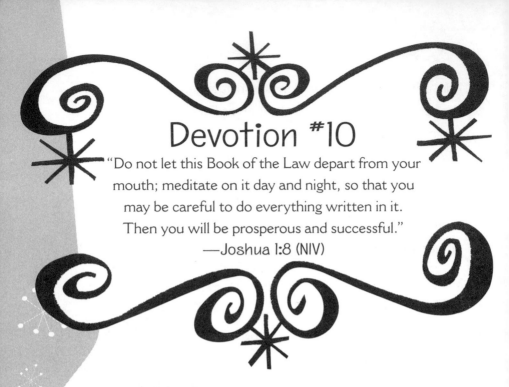

Devotion #10

"Do not let this Book of the Law depart from your mouth; meditate on it day and night, so that you may be careful to do everything written in it. Then you will be prosperous and successful."
—Joshua 1:8 (NIV)

FormuLa for Success

Keep reading and talking about God's Word. Think with careful attention, day and night, on all that is written in it. That way you'll be able to do the things it teaches. If you do, your days will be marked by peace and good fortune and favorable outcomes to your plans. That's God's formula: (1) Meditate. (2) Do what it says. (3) Be successful.

What's success? You want to have good relationships at home and at school. You want to succeed in your school work. You desire good outcomes on your soccer team or with your piano lessons. Success doesn't mean lots of money and cool clothes.

So if you're NOT being prosperous and successful, if your days are full of turmoil instead of peace—apply God's formula for success. Go to God's Word and find the answer to your problem. For example, are you out of cash, but you turn down all the neighbor's babysitting jobs so you can sleep late every morning? Study the ant in Proverbs 6:6, 8, 9 (NLT): "Take a lesson from the ants, you lazy fellow. Learn from their ways and be wise! They labor hard all summer . . . But you—all you do is sleep."

God's Word is jam-packed with words of wisdom on how to have a successful life. Study it carefully, do what you see written there, and look out! The blessings of peace, joy, success, and loving relationships will overflow.

Did You Know

. . . that a person who will not listen to wise advice will find poverty and shame? That a person who follows wise advice will find honor? (Proverbs 13:18 NASB)

More To Explore: Psalm 1:1–3 and Proverbs 11:12

GirL TaLk:

Are you getting into the Bible each day? Reading a chapter each day is a great way to learn what God wants for you. Just dive in, and God will speak to you.

God TaLk:

"Lord, I know you gave us the Bible to guide our lives. Please help me to learn what I need to learn. Help me to understand what you are saying to me through your Word. Amen."

Devotion #11

"But the fruit of the Spirit is love, joy, peace, patience, kindness, goodness, faithfulness, gentleness and self-control."—Galatians 5:22–23 (NIV)

Me Thinketh Some Fruit Stinketh!

Roadside fruit stands in the summertime are the result of healthy trees, cared for, pruned and sprayed by gardeners. The fruit of the Spirit (love, joy, peace, patience, kindness, goodness, faithfulness, gentleness, and self-control) is the result of a healthy human spirit cared for (and yes! pruned, and sprayed) by the Holy Spirit.

Does your "tree" produce rotten fruit sometimes instead? When your little brother makes you late for school, do you call him names? When someone accidentally steps on your toe in the lunch line, do you bite her head off? After school, do you devour the entire contents of the cookie jar? A short temper, a mean mouth, and a lack of self-control are NOT fruits of the Spirit.

Fruit doesn't appear overnight. You don't plant a skinny young tree and find ripe pears on it the next day. Fruit appears slowly. It's true of the fruit of the Spirit too. Do we produce this fruit all by ourselves? No. Jesus says, "Yes, I am the vine; you are the branches. Those who remain in me, and I in them, will produce much fruit. For apart from me you can do nothing." (John 15:5 NLT) Jesus living in you, through the power of the Holy Spirit, "grows" the fruit. Your part? Just hanging out on the vine!

The more you hang out with Jesus, the more you want to be like him. You're being patient when Little Brother makes you late, and you help him find his shoes. Or you just eat two cookies after school.

Doesn't a life filled with love, joy, peace, patience, kindness, goodness, faithfulness, gentleness, and self-control sound heavenly? People like to pick that kind of fruit!

Did You Know

. . . the apostle Paul considered love to be the greatest of these three: faith, hope, and love? See 1 Corinthians 13.

More To Explore: Matthew 12:33

Girl Talk:

How is your fruit? Is it fresh or does it reek? What one fruit do you think you need help with the most?

God Talk:

"Lord, I really want to grow in the fruit of the Spirit. Help me to be more like you. Amen."

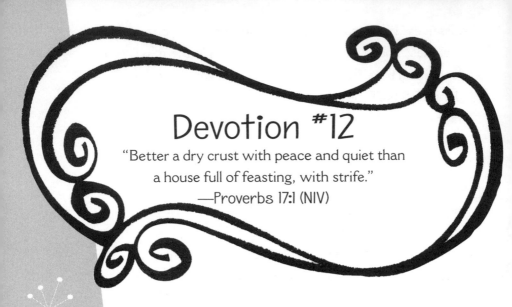

Devotion #12

"Better a dry crust with peace and quiet than
a house full of feasting, with strife."
—Proverbs 17:1 (NIV)

Go on a Strife Strike!

There's nothing worse than sitting down to a
mouth-watering meal and having an argument break
out at the table. Your stomach knots up, and the food sits
in your stomach like a rock. Who needs it? A dry crust of
bread eaten without stress or anxiety tastes better than steak
at a big party, if it comes with heated conflict.

Birthday parties and sleepovers can be fun and peaceful, but
sometimes quarrels break out. Girls make rude comments
about each other's clothes and hairstyles. They make fun of
other girls' clunky family cars or geeky siblings. You can be
surrounded with every type of party food imaginable,
but it's ruined by the strife-filled atmosphere.

Those caught in the middle of the fighting
often wish they'd never come. Hanging
out at home, eating toast and watching a
funny video with your family sounds like
a whole lot more fun. And it is!

The Bible says in Proverbs 15:17 that
it's better to share a meal of just veggies
where there is love than to eat some fancy

steaks in a room full of hate. Strife (fighting and violent arguments) open the door to all kinds of bad things in your life, like resentment, bitterness, and mean behavior. Nip it before it starts. And if you're with friends at lunch, when the strife strikes your group, get up and move. Get away from it. You might be surprised how many people follow you! No one enjoys being around someone who constantly picks fights. (Since we all have our crabby days, do a quick check and be sure that YOU aren't the quarrelsome person causing conflict for everyone else.)

Do what's necessary to be at peace within yourself. Then spread that peace to everyone you eat with. Make every meal a fun feast!

More To Explore: Proverbs 22:10

Did You Know

... the Bible says that if you don't forgive your friends, God won't forgive you? See Matthew 6:14–15. Any of us can cause strife, including you, so don't forget to forgive!

Girl Talk:

Think back to a recent time of strife, whether with friends or family. How did you handle it? How could you respond next time?

God Talk:

"Lord, help me walk in love, not strife. Please show me how to respond in these situations. Help me be a peacemaker in all of my relationships. I love you. Amen."

Devotion #13

"No matter what happens, always be thankful, for this is God's will for you who belong to Christ Jesus."—I Thessalonians 5:18 (NLT)

ATTiTude? GraTiTude!

Life happens when you've made other plans. But no matter what happens, God intends that we who belong to Christ should be grateful. Events are important, but God is even more interested in your attitude when things happen. Will your attitude be one of gratitude?

It's a cinch to be thankful on days the sun shines, our hair behaves perfectly, there's no school, and we're going shopping. Anyone in the world can be grateful on days like that. But can you be grateful no matter what happens? Like when your little sister pesters you, or it rains on the day of your birthday picnic? Believe it or not, *yes*, you can even be thankful then.

Sure, you may have to dig deep, but you can find something good in nearly every situation. The pesky sister wants to spend time with you because she loves you, right? Be thankful for that love. The rain on your picnic means you can do something even more creative, like picnic on top of your bunk bed—without the ants! But if it's something so bad or hurtful you just CAN'T see anything good in it, be thankful God loves you more than you can imagine and he's never going to leave your side.

As David wrote, "I will praise the LORD at all times. I will constantly speak his praises." (Psalm 34:1 NLT) Develop a thankful heart, one that looks every day for things to be grateful for. Then you'll find it much easier to be thankful when things happen that you don't like and didn't want. A heart full of gratitude to God is a joyful heart, no matter what happens.

Did You Know

. . . that in the time of King David, it was popular to give thanks to God by writing and singing songs of praise? Have you ever thanked God by singing to him?

More To Explore: Ephesians 5:20

Girl Talk:

Do you have a grateful heart? If not, do you desire to have a thankful heart?

God Talk:

"Lord, please develop a thankful heart within me. I praise you right now for all of the blessings in my life. I love you. Amen."

Devotion #14

"John replied, 'If you have two coats, give one to the poor. If you have food, share it with those who are hungry.'"—Luke 3:11 (NLT)

LeT IT Go!

Many people have more clothing and food than they truly need. In fact, most of us have closets crammed full of clothes and know at least three people who need to lose weight. If you have more than enough for your own needs, give some of it away. Many people—children and adults alike—have little money and few possessions. Share what you have with those who are cold and hungry.

Maybe you don't know anyone who is cold and hungry. But if you open your eyes and your heart, you'll see other needs. When you see a poor person standing in the rain at the bus stop, give her your umbrella. If your little tutoring pal is too poor to own any books, give him several stories from your own book shelf. Clean out your closets and donate your extra clothing to Goodwill. Maybe you don't have things to give away, but you could share your allowance or give away some of your babysitting money to someone in need. "Tell them to use their money to do good. They should be rich in good works and should give generously to those in need, always being ready to share with others whatever God has given them." (1 Timothy 6:18 NLT)

The next time you get annoyed at the mess in your closet, take an empty box and fill it with clothes you don't really need, clothes that someone else would love to have. Sharing what you have with the poor helps them—and the giving will bring you much joy.

Did You Know

. . . that in Bible times, clothing was made out of animal products such as sheep's wool and goat's hair? They probably itched a lot more than we do today in our cotton and rayon.

More To Explore: Matthew 25:31–46

Girl Talk:

How well do you do at sharing? Are there people in your life right now to whom you give your clothes, your time or your affection?

God Talk:

"Lord, I know I have lots I can share with others. Help me see the opportunities I have in front of me. Show me how to give with a loving heart.

Thank you for your loving example. Amen."

Mini-Quiz: (From Proverbs 25:21)

If your enemy is hungry, you should:

(a) throw a pie in his face.
(b) give a donation in his name to a soup kitchen.
(c) give him bread to eat.

(answer: c)

Devotion #15

"When you lie down, you will not be afraid;
when you lie down, your sleep will be sweet."
—Proverbs 3:24 (NIV)

ZZZZZZZZzzzzzz

Do you ever have trouble sleeping? When the lights go out, do your fears rush in to keep you awake? Maybe you IM'd with your friend instead of studying for that test, and you now fear flunking math. Or you've had a quarrel with your best friend, and you fear the relationship is over. Maybe you watched a horror video, and nightmares make sleep torture.

All kinds of fears can keep us awake, but Proverbs 3:24 says you *can* lie down without fear and that you should enjoy pleasant dreams.

We'd all love to have sweet dreams. But how do we sleep without fear? One way is how you spend your days. "Have two goals: wisdom—that is, knowing and doing right—and common sense. Don't let them slip away . . . With them on guard you can sleep without fear." Proverbs 4:21, 24 (LB)

In other words, be wise in how you spend your time, make good common sense decisions, and you'll sleep better.

Take practical steps to deal with the fears that ruin your sleep. Study for your math test, and fear of flunking won't keep you awake. Be kind and understanding instead of critical, and you won't have to be afraid of losing friends. Watch G-rated movies, and you won't have nightmares that keep you tossing and turning.

When you live wisely, making good decisions and using common sense, you will be able to say with the psalmist, "I will lie down and sleep in peace, for you alone, O LORD, make me dwell in safety." (Psalm 4:8 NIV) Good night, and sweet dreams!

Did You Know

. . . that new research suggests sleep may help us learn new motor skills? Remember that the next time you're having difficulty learning a new dance step or gymnastic flip.

More To Explore: Proverbs 6:22 (NIV)

Girl Talk:

Are you concerned about something so much that sleep seems far away? Write it down in a journal before bedtime, and ask God to give you peace about it. He will!

God Talk:

"Lord, I'm really scared about _____. I ask that you give me peace. I know you can handle all of my doubts and fears. Thank you for being with me always. Amen."

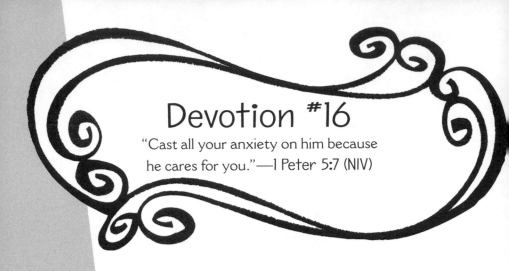

Devotion #16

"Cast all your anxiety on him because
he cares for you."—I Peter 5:7 (NIV)

No Fear Here!

Nobody likes to carry anxiety on her shoulders.
You know, that gut-twisting feeling inside when
you think your clothes look weird, or you dread being
called on in class when you don't know the answer.
Everyone has anxious thoughts, but the good news is that
you don't have to keep them!

You can cast your cares and worries on the Lord because
he's concerned for you and wants to help you. But you have
to mean it. None of this wishy-washy "giving your worries to
God" and grabbing them back a minute later. CAST your
anxieties on him—throw them with great force so they
stay put. Get rid of them!

Anxiety can attack whenever you have to
perform, like in a concert or before a ball
game. Most girls feel anxious when doing
something different, like meeting new
people or trying to ice skate for the first
time. But anxiety can also attack when
you're reading a book or watching a
movie, and something reminds you of a
bad time in your past. You have personal

concerns, family cares, worries about the present, and worries about the future.

The cure is to cast your worries and anxieties on God, and leave every circumstance and event to him. You do that in prayer. Tell God you're throwing your worries onto him and that you don't want them back. Believe that he has every situation under control, that he sees your need and is willing to meet it. Trust that he will help you play that piece in the concert and smile at the strange faces in your new home room.

Don't carry your anxieties and worries a minute longer. Wind up, take aim, and throw those cares away!

Did You Know

. . . the disciples were afraid of a fierce storm, even though Jesus was right there in the boat with them? Read Mark 4:38–41.

More To Explore: Philippians 4:6

GirL TaLk:

Do you focus on the bad stuff that comes your way, or do you look to the future for good things to come?

God TaLk:

"Lord, you know all my worries and fears. I give them to you, each and every one. Thank you for caring about my every thought and feeling. Amen."

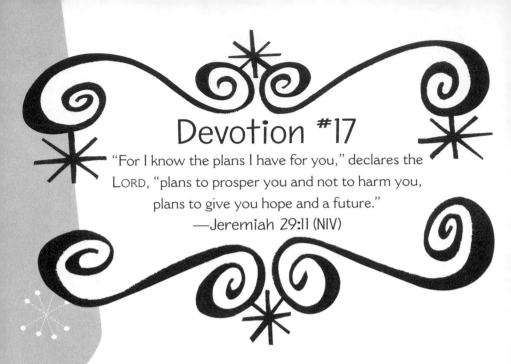

Devotion #17

"For I know the plans I have for you," declares the LORD, "plans to prosper you and not to harm you, plans to give you hope and a future."
—Jeremiah 29:11 (NIV)

Dream a Big Dream

God has a plan for your life, and it's a good plan to help you grow stronger and be successful. We sometimes fear God's plan will hurt us, or keep us from having something we truly desire. But we can have hope for the future. God has promised he will meet our needs and give us each what is best.

All girls dream about the future. Maybe you dream of breaking your school's hurdles record or getting the lead in the fall musical. Maybe your career goals include a scholarship to a music school or becoming a scientist to cure cancer. Whatever your dreams are, they may not just be *your* ideas. God may have placed them in your heart.

Make goals, and take steps to go after them. Trust that your dreams are from God, and ask him to change them if he has a different plan for your life. If he does, you can always trust that his plan is a better one! He's had it all under control from the beginning. "You saw me before I was born. Every day of my life was recorded in your book. Every moment was laid out before a single day had passed." (Psalm 139:16 NLT)

Because God also gave us free will, begin taking little steps toward reaching your dreams and goals. First, talk to God about them. Ask him to change anything about your goals that he wants to change. Then break your future goals into smaller steps you can begin now. Study. Practice. Learn. Reach for excellence. Then you will be ready to fulfill God's plans to prosper you in the wonderful future that lies ahead.

Did You Know

. . . King David's goal was to build the temple for the Lord? God told him that his off-spring would build it instead. Even David had to change his dreams sometimes! (2 Samuel 7)

More To Explore: Psalm 139:17

Girl Talk:

Do you trust God with your dreams? How would you feel if he told you that his dreams for you were different than yours?

God Talk:

"Lord, I trust you with my dreams. I know you have a great future for me, and I'm excited about it! Thank you for helping me accomplish my dreams. Amen."

Devotion #18

"You made all the delicate, inner parts of my body
and knit me together in my mother's womb.
Thank you for making me so wonderfully complex!
Your workmanship is marvelous—and how well
I know it."—Psalm 139:13-14 (NLT)

An Inside Job

Imagine God carefully forming you inside your mother's body, putting together all your miniature inward parts. He created each tiny organ, bone and muscle, then linked them together in a pattern that created you. What a miracle! You are hand crafted by God himself.

If this is true, then why do girls worry about being too fat or too thin? Maybe you fret about your size eight feet, ears that poke out, squinty eyes, or pointy nose. We fall into the deadly trap of comparing ourselves to others, then envying how they look. Your body image (or how you see yourself) may not be based on the facts. You can feel too skinny, yet look beautiful to everyone else. Most important, you always look beautiful to God! He carefully molded you to look *exactly* like you do.

It's fine to want to appear your best. Wash your hair often, press your wrinkled blouse, and wear clothing styles that flatter you. But don't forget—while people notice the outside of you, God studies your heart. If you really want to change how you feel about your looks, start on the inside. See yourself through God's eyes, the one who so carefully made you and loves you. He says you are marvelous and complex!

Once you begin to see yourself as perfectly as God sees you, it will show! Your confidence will shine—and the work you've done inside will be visible on the outside.

Did You Know

. . . that by all appearances, David should have been wiped out by Goliath? He was young, not that tall, and went to battle with no armor! Read 1 Samuel 17.

More To Explore: 1 Peter 3:3-4

Girl Talk:

How often do you worry about your appearance? Can you give this worry to God? Do you believe he cares?

God Talk:

"Lord, I know you created every part of me, and you don't make mistakes. Help me to be content with every aspect of who I am. Thank you for loving me. Amen."

Beauty 101:

To help keep your body working well and looking good, try climbing stairs and doing push-ups and sit-ups for fifteen minutes total, three to five days a week.

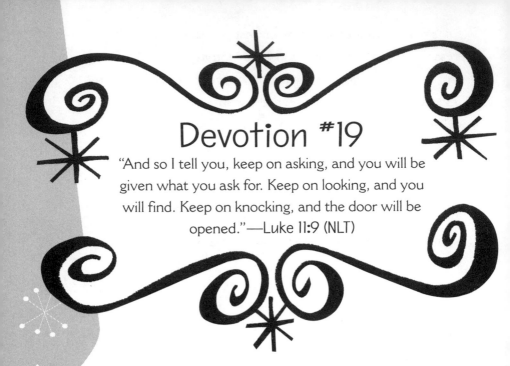

Devotion #19

"And so I tell you, keep on asking, and you will be given what you ask for. Keep on looking, and you will find. Keep on knocking, and the door will be opened."—Luke 11:9 (NLT)

Seek and Find

Have you ever been on a scavenger hunt? The list of items to find is long, and sometimes you look a long time before you find an item. Prayer can be like that. God promises that if we keep on asking, we'll be given what we need. If we keep searching for answers, we'll find them.

Can you ask for and receive *anything* you desire? Probably not. No matter how many times you ask your parents for a car of your own, you won't get one until you're old enough to drive safely. That's because they love you and want to protect you. God, your heavenly Father, is the same.

As you look for God's answers, one of two things will happen. God may give you what you asked for, or he may change your desire *as you spend time with him*. You may lose your desire for what you've been praying for. God will

change your desire to match what he wants to give you—
something much better than what you asked for in the
first place.

Talk to God about what you want and need, and be
patient. God's timing is perfect—but it's nearly always
slower than we wish. Look in God's Word for your
answers. "If any of you lacks wisdom, let him ask of God,
who gives to all liberally and without reproach, and it will
be given to him." James 1:5 (NKJV)

Ask. Look. Knock. Be patient. Then watch the doors
swing open as your prayers are answered!

Did You Know

. . . that Maggie, one of the
Corn Flakes, is seeking? She
doesn't want what the
popular girls offer, but she's
not sure what she's missing.
Root for her in *Sophie's
World*.

More To Explore: 1 John 3:21–22

GirL TaLk:

Do you ask God for what
you need? How confident
are you that God will
answer your prayers?

God TaLk:

"Lord, I know I need to ask you for
what I need. Help me to see what you want
me to see. Show me the doors you want
me to knock on. Amen."

Devotion #20

"Jesus answered, 'I am the way and the truth and the life. No one comes to the Father except through me.'"—John 14:6 (NIV)

The Most Important Decision

A Jewish religious leader named Nicodemus asked Jesus how he could get to heaven. Jesus said Nicodemus needed to be born again, and that Jesus was the only way to get to heaven. He said no one could come to the Father, God, except through his Son. Jesus is the way, the truth, and the life. Today some people might seek "the way" through astrology. Others try to find "truth" by going to fortune tellers. Some try to find "life" by owning expensive things or hurting their bodies by being dangerously thin. But Jesus is the only way, the only truth, and the only life.

In Romans 3:23, God's Word says our sin—our wrong attitudes and actions—has separated us from God. Because of that, we deserve to be separated from God forever. "For the wages of sin is death, but the free gift of God is eternal life in Christ Jesus our Lord." (Romans 6:23 NASB) How did God make this free gift available to us? "For God so loved the world that he gave his only Son, so that everyone who believes in him will not perish but have eternal life." (John 3:16 NLT)

Have you made the decision to ask God to forgive your sins? Have you accepted Jesus as your Savior? *It's the most important decision of your life.* If you would like to receive Jesus as your Savior now, pray the following prayer.

"God, I know you sent your Son to die for my sins. Thank you for Jesus. You know my sins—please forgive them. Thank you for making me a new person in Jesus. I want him to live in my heart today. I ask this in his name. Amen."

Did You Know

. . . that 2 Corinthians 5:17 says that when you become a Christian, you become a new creature? Cool!

More To Explore: Romans 5:8, 10 and I John 4:9-10

GirL TaLk:

Do you have a friend who might not know the steps to salvation? How could you share the way to heaven with your friend?

God TaLk:

"Lord, help me to walk with you all the days of my life. Thank you for giving your life for me. I love you. Amen."

Devotion #21

"If we say we have no sin, we are only fooling ourselves and refusing to accept the truth. But if we confess our sins to [God], he is faithful and just to forgive us and to cleanse us from every wrong."—1 John 1:8–9 (NLT)

Heavenly Soap

No one but God is perfect, but sometimes we fool ourselves into thinking we're not so bad. After all, we don't steal or tell big lies or cheat like *some* people we know. Does that mean we have no sin? No! In fact, if we claim to be perfect—doing exactly what God wants us to do in every situation—we are only fooling ourselves. Instead, admit your sins to God. You can count on him to freely forgive you and wash your spirit clean.

Maybe you didn't steal or cheat today, but God is interested in your attitudes and thoughts as well as your behavior. Did you tell a classmate, "Pretty outfit" while you were thinking, "Ugly rag"? Did you shove your little brother out of the way when he stood in front of the refrigerator? These things fall short of the standard Christians should live up to.

You're not alone. We all fall short sometimes. Thankfully, God has provided a way to wash that dirt from our hearts and spirits. Be humble. Admit where you fell short, and specifically name the sins you want forgiveness for. Not "I'm sorry I missed the mark today, God." Instead, "God, please forgive me for being disrespectful and mouthy to my dad." Being specific will help you to avoid repeating that sin. Then trust God that you are totally forgiven.

We bathe because we've had contact with dirt in our world and need to be washed. Take time to confess your sins daily too, and go to bed at night with both body and spirit squeaky clean.

Did You Know

. . . that the word "prodigal" means recklessly extravagant? The parable of the prodigal son is a great example of first falling short and then receiving forgiveness. Read Luke 15:11–32.

More To Explore: Jeremiah 2:22

Girl Talk:

What sin do you have pressing on your heart right now? Have you asked God forgiveness for that sin?

God Talk:

"Lord, I know I fail your expectations every day. Please forgive me for

_____. Thank you for always being ready to forgive. Amen."

Devotion #22

"Yet I am always with you; you hold me by
my right hand."—Psalm 73:23 (NIV)

In His Grip

Sometimes—at school, at home, at a friend's
sleepover—we are hit with the fearful thought: "I
don't belong here, and I don't fit in." We aren't alone,
but we feel lonely just the same. At times like these,
remember that you still belong to God. He always accepts
you. In fact, he's holding on to your hand so you can't get
lost and are never alone.

You might feel lonely because you actually spend a lot of time
alone. Maybe your parents get home late, so you're by yourself
after school for a few hours. Or there is tension and fighting
where you live, so you spend hours alone in your room to
escape it. Maybe you spend Saturdays alone because no
friends live nearby, or you need to babysit and help
your mom. At those times too, remember that
you're never really alone. God has a firm grip
on your hand. Talk to him. Tell him you're
lonely. Ask God to fill that lonely place in
your heart. He will!

Being lonely can make you depressed
and dismayed, but help is on the way!
"Don't be afraid, for I am with you. Do not

be dismayed, for I am your God. I will strengthen you. I will help you. I will uphold you with my victorious right hand." (Isaiah 41:10 NLT) Sometimes God will fill your heart with so much love that your loneliness just disappears. You can't explain it; it just melts away. Sometimes he sends people to you—in person, on the phone, through e-mail or Instant Messaging—to meet your need for company. He will meet your need in different ways at different times.

No matter what happens, remember that you're not alone. You always belong to God. He has your hand firmly in his grasp, and he will never let go.

Did You Know

. . . even Faithgirlz! feel lonely sometimes? Sophie feels so lonely she asks God for a friend who understands her. Find out who appears in *Sophie's World*.

More To Explore:

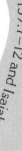

Psalm 139:7–12 and Isaiah 41:13

Girl Talk:

Have you felt lonely in the past week? What can you do when you feel this way?

God Talk:

"Lord, I am feeling really alone right now. I know you are always there. Please help me to remember I can always call on you. Amen."

Devotion #23

"My mouth shall speak wisdom, and the meditation of my heart shall give understanding."—Psalm 49:3 (NKJV)

A True Wise Guy

We all feel embarrassed when dumb things fall out of our mouths and make us look stupid, thoughtless, or clueless. It doesn't have to be that way. If you study what your Bible says and try to follow its principles, you can speak with wisdom. Thinking carefully (or meditating) on those verses tucked away in your heart will lead to understanding. You'll grow in good judgment and common sense.

Wisdom and understanding will keep you from all kinds of problems. Do you have trouble controlling your tongue when your mom tells you to get off the phone? Do you use your lunch money to buy chocolate candy, leaving you without a lunch? Are you sometimes embarrassed at the mall by the behavior of your loud friends? God's Word says something definite about each of those. Meditate on those verses, and you will understand what to do.

Sometimes the silly things that pop out of our mouths mean nothing. We all have those days when our brain seems to go on vacation. But if you want sensible things to come out of your mouth, you need to program your brain with good food—God's Word. Your brain is like a super-computer, and what you feed into it is what will come out. Feed it junk movies, books and TV, and count on junk coming back out. Feed it a steady diet of God's Word, and just watch those pearls of wisdom you have to share. Let God's Word get deep in your hearts, for "whatever is in your heart determines what you say." (Matthew 12:34)

Clueless chick or wise woman? The choice is yours!

Did You Know

. . . a plant with no roots dies when bad weather comes along. If you have no "roots" in God's Word, you will shrivel up when problems come your way. Read more in Mark 4:1–21.

More To Explore: James 1:5

Girl Talk:

Think of the last time you embarrassed yourself by the way you acted or what you said. Did you stop and ask God to help you?

God Talk:

(From Psalm 19:14 NLT) "May the words of my mouth and the thoughts of my heart be pleasing to you, O Lord, my rock and my redeemer. Amen."

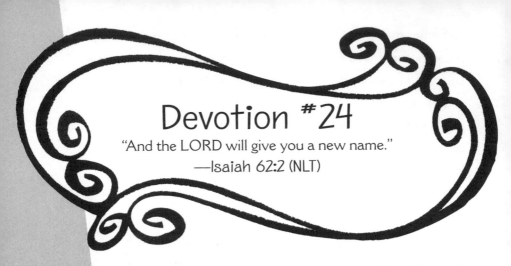

Devotion #24

"And the LORD will give you a new name."
—Isaiah 62:2 (NLT)

What's In a Name?

Ever wish you could change your name? Maybe your nickname suited you at one time, but now you want something more grown-up than what your parents call you (Sunshine or Pumpkin). Even worse, sometimes we are branded at school with negative nicknames, like Squirrel, Dumbo, or Chubbette. It's exciting to know that God has given you a new and special name!

Today most new parents choose to name their baby something that is currently popular, or they carry on a family name for many generations. However, in biblical times, names were nearly always chosen for a special reason. Each name stood for a character quality or told something about the person. When God called his people into a new and closer relationship, he often gave them new names to "announce" this change to the world. Abram became Abraham, Sarai became Sarah, Jacob became Israel, and Saul became Paul. Each of these famous Bible people lived up to the new name given to them by God.

What people call us affects how we feel about ourselves. A complimentary nickname gives us a boost and makes us smile. A negative nickname makes us want to hide. If you don't like the nickname others have given you, choose a new one for yourself. Ask family members to update your nickname, and start calling yourself by your new name. Sign your letters and e-mails that way. Let the old name—and the old you—be a thing of the past.

So what *is* God's new name for you? He calls you Beloved, Chosen, a child of the King. Your name is so important to him that it's written in the Lamb's Book of Life.

Did You Know

. . . that the rhyme "Sticks and stones may break my bones, but words will never hurt me" is totally untrue? Broken bones heal, but words can wound a heart or self-image forever. See Proverbs 12:18.

More To Explore: Genesis 17:5 and 32:28

Girl Talk:

Have you ever been called a nasty name? How did it make you feel? On the flip side, ask forgiveness for any names you have called others.

God Talk:

"Lord, I thank you for calling me Beloved. Please help me to remember that my value lies in you, not in what others think of me. Amen."

Devotion #25

"Meanwhile, Zacchaeus stood there and said to the
Lord, 'I will give half my wealth to the poor, Lord,
and if I have overcharged people on their taxes,
I will give them back four times as much!'"
—Luke 19:8 (NLT)

From Taker To Giver

When Zacchaeus met Jesus, it changed him from a
cheating tax collector into a generous giver. He was sorry for
his selfishness and proved it by giving half his money to the
poor. He even went to those he'd cheated and paid them
back four times more than he'd stolen from them.

Zacchaeus became a radical giver! He went beyond just
paying back what he took. For the first time, he saw
the needs of others and chose to be a "giver." You
can bet he went from being a hated man to a
loved one.

How much do you enjoy being around
the girl at school who constantly lets
you pay for the movie rentals and soda
every week, while she keeps her money
for her own shopping trips? Self-centered
takers are no fun to be around. It's normal to

want to see that our needs get met, but we need to look out for the needs of others, too.

Make a change in your thinking. Look at the people in your life and ask yourself, "What can I give *you* or do for *you*?" Become a radical giver. Besides helping others, joy will flood your own heart. "Yes, you will be enriched so that you can give even more generously. And when we take your gifts to those who need them, they will break out in thanksgiving to God." (2 Corinthians 9:11 NLT)

If you tend to be a taker with your friends and family members, turn your life around. Be a giver. It will transform your relationships—and your life.

Did You Know

. . . that a poor widow gave so much more to the church than a very rich man? Read about her gift in Luke 21:1–4.

More To Explore:

Acts 20:35 and Deuteronomy 15:7–11

Girl Talk:

What do you have that you could give to others? Is it hard for you to give, without expecting anything in return?

God Talk:

"Lord, I thank you for all you give to me. I want to give to others, without thinking of myself. Thank you for helping me give with a loving heart. Amen."

Devotion #26

"Work hard and cheerfully at whatever you do,
as though you were working for the Lord
rather than for people."—Colossians 3:23 (NLT)

Get a New Boss

Whatever job you have before you—washing dishes, babysitting for the neighbors, mowing the lawn—do it with excellence and without grumbling. Your employer may pay you, but the Lord is really your boss. Work just as hard for your employer as you would if Jesus were standing next to you, watching.

When you babysit, do you play with the children, or do you plunk them down in front of the TV so you can gab on the phone with your friends? When doing yard work for a customer, do you work hard when he's around, but when he leaves, sit in the shade and drink soda? God sees you cheating your employer by resting on the job.

Work hard and cheerfully, remembering that your true boss is there beside you. Perhaps, though, your problem is the opposite. Even when you do an excellent job, some people are impossible to please. A cranky critic will find fault with some tiny thing, even if ninety-nine percent of your work is superb. In cases like this, remember that you're working for a new boss—the Lord—and not for this judgmental person. Keep doing an excellent job, but remember that your worth and value is not in what you do, but in who you are as belonging to Christ.

The next time you agree to do a job for someone—for payment or not—remember that you're really working for the Lord. Your new boss is standing right beside you, to help you and strengthen you as you cheerfully do your best.

Did You Know

. . . that Joseph was such a great employee that he went from being a slave to Pharaoh's right-hand man? Read his story in Genesis 37, 39–41.

God Talk:

"Lord, I thank you for the jobs you send my way. Help me to do them with a cheerful heart. Amen."

More To Explore: Ephesians 6:5–7 and Colossians 3:17

Girl Talk:

Have you done any paying or non-paying jobs lately? Do you feel proud of your work? Does it make a difference that God is always watching your efforts?

Mini-Quiz

1. T/F Parents have authority to punish their children.
2. T/F As a child, Jesus did not submit (yield) to his earthly parents, Mary and Joseph.

1. T   2. F

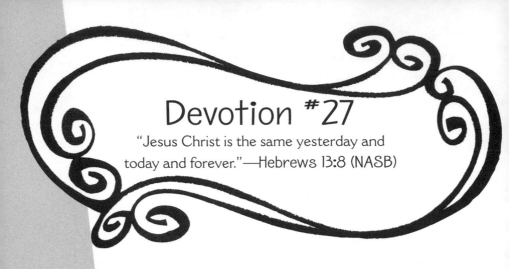

Devotion #27

"Jesus Christ is the same yesterday and today and forever."—Hebrews 13:8 (NASB)

Jesus Never Goes Out of Style

Fashion trends change so quickly that sometimes they're over before you've had the latest layered haircut or bought the coolest shoes or found that mini handbag in fake leather. Movies that are popular this year will be in the video sale bin next year. Trendy restaurants and fabulous foods change from month to month. The world is constantly shifting, but one person never changes: Jesus. He's the same today as he's always been, and he'll be that way forever.

The more you read the Word of God, the more things you find out about Jesus. He's the Good Shepherd guiding and protecting us, he's the Great Physician healing us, he's our Rock to stand firmly upon, he's the Way, the Truth and the Life. He loves children and wants them to come to him. He's the Bread of Life. He always has been. He always will be.

Not all the people in our lives can be counted on like that. Friends move away or find new best friends. Favorite teachers and pastors retire. Sometimes parents leave, or a grandparent dies. In a world that is constantly changing, be thankful that Jesus is the same today as he always was— and that you can count on him for all your tomorrows. He has promised to never leave you, and (unlike people some-times) he always tells the truth.

When your life seems to change every week, it can be very unsettling if you look at the circumstances. Instead, look up. Look to Jesus. You can walk confidently through any changes life throws at you as long as you stick close to the One who always stays the same. "For I am the LORD, I do not change." (Malachi 3:6 NKJV)

Did You Know

. . . that it's perfectly normal to feel awkward about your body changes? You are going through puberty. You might also experience moodiness and struggle with who you are. Feeling weird is normal!

More To Explore: James 1:7

Girl Talk:

Have you had changes happen to your body? How do you feel about these changes?

God Talk:

"Lord, I know there will be changes all through my lifetime. Help me to look to you when changes come. Thank you for never changing. I love you. Amen."

Devotion #28

"But seek first his kingdom and his righteousness, and all these things will be given to you as well."—Matthew 6:33 (NIV)

First Things First

Do you spend a lot of your time trying to get things —food, cool clothes, and decorations—for your room or locker? If so, you probably have little time left over to do those things God may want you to do. If that's the case, you have it backwards. God's Word says that if we will make living for the Lord our *first* concern, he will *give* us all we need from day to day. Stop chasing after material possessions. Focus on the kingdom of God, and let the things chase you!

For example, do you wish you had more friends? Instead of working hard to impress people or buy friendship with flattery or gifts, seek God instead. Ask him how you can meet someone else's need for friendship, how you can show his love to people. As you focus on living for God, he will provide you with friends. And they will be true, loyal friends—not the fickle kind you can buy.

Or do you wish you had more money to buy things you need? Then do things

God's way. First give some money away to a person who needs it. God will then provide for your own needs, often in a way you least expect it. "If you give, you will receive. Your gift will return to you in full measure, pressed down, shaken together to make room for more, and running over." Luke 6:38 (NLT)

Put first things first. Live your life to be pleasing to the Lord, and don't worry about getting things. Shift your focus. Make living for God the main thing, and he will see that you have everything you need.

Did You Know

. . . the Faithgirlz! find out that, by asking God first, their needs get met? Maggie helps meet Sophie's need after Sophie prays about it in *Sophie's World.*

More To Explore: Matthew 13:44–46 and Psalm 34:9–10

GirL TaLk:

Are you putting first things first? What is at the top of your priority list? Where do you put God on your list?

God TaLk:

"Lord, I know I have lots of things on my mind that really don't matter. Please help me to put you first in my life. I want you to matter the most! Amen."

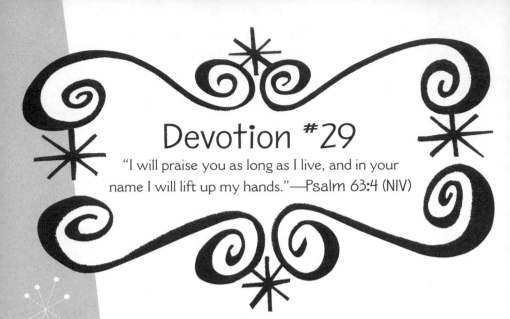

Devotion #29

"I will praise you as long as I live, and in your
name I will lift up my hands."—Psalm 63:4 (NIV)

Finding Your Faith Fit

We are to bless and honor and respect God our whole
lives. One way we show this praise is to raise our hands
toward heaven in song and prayer. You may think that lifting
your hands during worship is a "modern" or contemporary
kind of worship. But David talked about it many times in the
Psalms. "Hear the voice of my supplications when I cry to
You, when I lift up my hands toward Your holy sanctuary."
(Psalm 28:2 KJV) And "Let my prayer be set before You
as incense, the lifting up of my hands as the evening
sacrifice." (Psalm 141:2 KJV)

We all prefer places where we feel comfortable, where there's a good fit with our sur-
roundings and we know the routine. That
isn't always the case—even in church. If
you visit a different church on vacation or
with a friend, you may find their customs
make you very uncomfortable. Do they
raise their hands when singing or praying?

That might be new to you—even a bit scary.

There are different kinds of worship styles because there are different types of people. You might be shy or more quiet, preferring to pray with your eyes closed, head bowed, and hands in your lap. Or you might feel freer, raising your hands in praise to God during singing and prayer time. There is no right or wrong. It's a matter of comfort. You should never feel pressured to make a worship style "fit" though. It's a personal thing. Don't force it. Let God be your guide.

Pray and worship in whatever manner makes you feel most comfortable. Remember, God looks on the heart, so you don't have to raise your hands for him to see your love for him.

Did You Know

. . . the Psalms were written to be sung? Some even have notes that say "to the director of music." They had choir directors back then too!

More To Explore: Psalm 104:33; 145:1–3

Girl Talk:

What do you like about your church's services? Do you ever feel uncomfortable in church? How do you like to praise God in private?

God Talk:

"Thank you, Lord, that I can freely worship you. Thank you for teaching me ways to worship that I am comfortable with and that please you. Amen."

Devotion #30

"The Lord himself goes before you and will be with you; he will never leave you nor forsake you. Do not be afraid; do not be discouraged."
—Deuteronomy 31:8 (NIV)

No Fear Here!

What a comfort to know that we are never alone, that in every scary situation the Lord himself goes before us to mark out a safe path, then walks us through it. We don't need to let discouragement stop us, and we never need to turn and run in fear. If the God and Creator of the whole universe goes ahead of us and stays with us forever, what should we be afraid of? The more you trust God's Word and spend time talking with the Lord, the less fear you will feel.

Fears come in all shapes and sizes. You might experience fear of the dark, ferocious dogs, or crashing thunderstorms. Most people fear performances, whether it's a dance recital or giving a book report in class. Maybe your fears are even bigger, like fear of parents divorcing or fear that a sick grandparent won't recover. Will God be there through it all? Absolutely!

Sometimes we're afraid of other people:

the bully on the school bus who threatens you, the strange looking man at the bus stop, even your principal! Whatever your fear, the answer is the same. "For He Himself has said, 'I will never leave you nor forsake you.' So we may boldly say: 'The LORD is my helper; I will not fear. What can man do to me?'" (Hebrews 13:4–6 NKJV)

Whatever your fear is—you don't have to be afraid anymore. God says in Isaiah 41:13, "For I am the LORD, your God, who takes hold of your right hand and says to you, do not fear; I will help you."

So don't worry, and don't fear. He will help you make it through every fearful situation you face.

Did You Know

. . . that even angels can cause people to be frightened because they're so big and divine? It seems angels in the Bible are always saying, "Fear not!" when they appear to people. Read Luke 2:8–11.

More To Explore: 1 Chronicles 28:20 and Isaiah 43:1–2

Girl Talk:

What sort of things make you feel afraid? Have you asked God to free you from those fears?

God Talk:

"Lord, I'm afraid of

_____, and I want to be free from that fear. I give it to you. Thank you for never leaving my side. Amen."

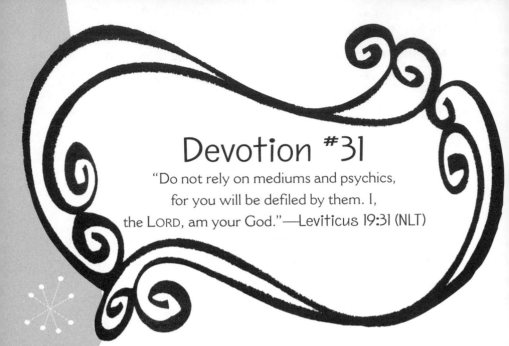

Devotion #31

"Do not rely on mediums and psychics,
for you will be defiled by them. I,
the LORD, am your God."—Leviticus 19:31 (NLT)

Who Ya Gonna Call?

A Ouija board, palm reading, horoscopes, fortune tellers—just a harmless way to have fun at birthday parties and sleepovers? No way! God's Word specifically warns us against trusting anyone who claims to contact the dead, tell the future, or see into the spiritual realm for information not available to the rest of us. Why the warning? You will be stained (and wrongly directed) by them. If you want wisdom and insight for making decisions, go to the Lord instead, who is your God.

Some innocent-looking things are traps, devices to hook you into much more serious forms of witchcraft. Some people invite fortune tellers, palm readers, Tarot card readers, and psychics to parties for entertainment. Newspapers and magazines carry horoscopes. Psychics have TV shows complete with hotlines. They promise to predict your future or give you spiritual advice about a decision you're facing. They've been around for thousands of years, and the Bible has a lot to say about avoiding them.

God understands that you need help making decisions. You want to make choices that will have a positive affect on your future. But don't go to psychics and fortune tellers. Go directly to God instead. "If you need wisdom—if you want to know what God wants you to do—ask him, and he will gladly tell you. He will not resent your asking." (James 1:5 NLT)

If you want true help for your future, go to the Bible for answers, and pray directly to God. You can't go wrong there!

Did You Know

. . . God considered every part of the occult an "abomination" (vile, shameful action) and it's forbidden? That includes people who try to talk to spirits and those who practice witchcraft. (Deuteronomy 18:9–14)

More To Explore: Leviticus 20:6

GirL TaLk:

Ever read horoscopes in a magazine or wanted to call a psychic hotline? Do you know that God has all of the answers and wisdom you'll ever need?

God TaLk:

"Lord, I trust you for direction in my life. I know I don't need to consult anyone else. I just want to follow you. Amen."

Devotion #32

"You are like babies who drink only milk and cannot eat solid food. And a person who is living on milk isn't very far along in the Christian life and doesn't know much about doing what is right. Solid food is for those who are mature, who have trained themselves to recognize the difference between right and wrong and then do what is right."
—Hebrews 5:12–14 (NLT)

Something To Chew On

Accepting Jesus as your personal Savior is the *beginning* of your Christian journey, not the end. Be determined to grow in your Christian walk. After you've been a believer for a long time, you should be sharing with others about Jesus. Instead, many believers have to be taught the basics of salvation and repentance over and over again. That's like a baby who never grows up, who never goes on from milk to solid food. Study God's Word, and let godly parents, pastors, and Sunday school teachers train you to know the difference between right and wrong. Then do what you know is right.

Have you been around a baby brother or sister or cousin? Then you've seen them go from milk to solid food—a big sign of growing up physically. Wouldn't it look odd to see your sister still drinking bottles at age eight or eighteen? God says we are to grow up spiritually too.

How can you tell if you're still a baby spiritually? You can be very brave and ask others if there are areas of your life when you act babyish or immature. Or pay attention to the times your parents say, "How many times do I have to tell you . . . ?" Maybe it's to stop fighting with your brother or get to school on time. Being a peacemaker and exercising self-control would be good areas to grow in.

Make it your goal to grow up, not just physically, but spiritually as well.

Did You Know

. . . that a baby Christian is compared to a small boat on rocky seas? See Ephesians 4:14.

More To Explore: 1 Peter 2:2

Girl Talk:

Is there one area in your life that you especially want to work on? Ask God for help.

God Talk:

"Lord, I know I have a lot to learn about the Christian life. I really need help with

_____.

I ask for your guidance as I try to become closer to you. Amen."

Beauty 101:

As you work on your inner beauty, keep track of how you're changing with a chart or a journal. It's encouraging to look back and see your progress!

Devotion #33

"And I want women to be modest in their appearance. They should wear decent and appropriate clothing and not draw attention to themselves by the way they fix their hair or by wearing gold or pearls or expensive clothes."
—I Timothy 2:9 (NLT)

Fashion Statements

It seems like wherever we look—in TV, movies, magazines, music videos, and clothing stores—we're bombarded with examples of indecent clothing. We see so many bare bellies and super-short skirts that we can start to think it looks cool—instead of cheap. How we dress sends a message to others about how we value ourselves.

You're a child of God, and this needs to show in how you dress. You can still be in style! But choose clothing that covers you and isn't so tight or short that it draws attention to your body. Dress nicely and fix your hair, but watch for excessive pride that says you must have certain brands of expensive shoes and clothing.

It's possible to see so many bad clothing

examples that you become blind to it. It seems normal and somehow okay. It's not. If you question whether a piece of clothing is too immodest or indecent, get a second opinion. Your friends, who are exposed to the same shows and ads you are, will not be your best source of a godly opinion. Be brave, and ask your mom or youth leader. They will be honest with you and help you find other choices that are fashionable and pretty, yet modest. The Holy Spirit will help you too.

You were bought with a price. You are of infinite value to God. Does the fashion statement you make with your clothes show this truth?

Did You Know

. . . that the color purple used to be the color of royalty? Even godly Proverbs women wore purple and fine linen. See Proverbs 31:22.

More To Explore: 1 Peter 3:3–4

Girl Talk:

Think back to the last few items of clothing you bought. Would God approve of them? Do you realize the message your clothing sends?

God Talk:

"Lord, I want to send the right message with what I wear. Help me to choose wisely and modestly. Thank you that you care about every detail of my life. Amen."

Beauty 101:

Buy clothes that fit, but are slightly loose. You're growing, so something that looks great today may not be modest in a couple months!

Devotion #34

"Finally, I confessed all my sins to you and stopped trying to hide them. I said to myself, 'I will confess my rebellion to the LORD.' And you forgave me! All my guilt is gone."—Psalm 32:5 (NLT)

What Are You Hiding?

Come clean with God. Tell him the sins you commit each day. Stop trying to cover them up. Instead, admit you've refused to do what God's Word said to do because you just wanted your own way instead. Admit it, and God will forgive and free you from all your regret. Your guilt—that vague uneasiness that you've done something wrong—will be gone.

We may fall short every day, but we often do things with our sins other than confess them. We make excuses for ourselves. ("I shouldn't have smarted off to my mom, but I'm just so tired.") We cover it up. (We hide a new shirt in the back of the closet, the one we bought instead of the school book we needed.) We "forget" the sin. (After gossiping about our friend, we cover the guilty feeling by quickly focusing on a TV show.) Do the sins go away, along with the consequences? No. Your mom is still mad. You still need that book for class. Your friend is hurt when the gossip gets back to her.

When you carry around un-confessed sin, it's like hiding some forbidden food in your room. It's "out of sight, out of mind" for a while—until it spoils and starts to stink. Sin doesn't stay hidden forever either. Even if it did—if no other human being found out—God knows.

So 'fess up! It will remove the guilt from your conscience, give you peace in your heart, and spark a determination not to do that thing again.

Did You Know

. . . Sophie goes through this same conflict in *Sophie's World?* She's bothered by the way she acted, and that feeling continues until she asks God for help.

More To Explore: 2 Samuel 24:10 and Psalm 86:5

Girl Talk:

Do you have sin that is hidden away in your heart? Tell it all to God and ask for forgiveness.

God Talk:

"Lord, I have done something I'm not proud of, and I need to confess it to you. I'm so sorry I

_____.

I don't want to do it again. Thank you for forgiving me every time I ask. Amen."

Devotion #35

"But let all who take refuge in you be glad;
let them ever sing for joy."—Psalm 5:11 (NIV)

Count It All Joy

A refuge is a safe place, protected from attack or violent storms. It's a place you can run to, and you'll be safe as long as you stay there. God is our refuge too. When you're going through tough times, when you're afraid, he's the best place to go for shelter. Not only will you be safe, but you'll be so relieved that you'll sing for joy!

We don't always run to God for help or shelter when we're going through trouble. You might eat a candy bar when upset, or go shopping, or zone out with a gripping movie. Will that help? Not really. You might forget your troubles for a short time, but you won't feel happy or cheerful for long. That only comes—and stays—when you seek shelter from your dangers or hardships by going to God, in his Word and in prayer. Then you'll feel true peace and joy that will last.

Sometimes, before you actually feel the joy, you have to praise and worship

God by faith. In other words, you praise him when you don't really feel like it. If you sing songs that praise God, or listen to upbeat praise music—especially when you are sad or discouraged—you'll get back your joy.

If you run to God for safety from the storms in your life, if you choose to be cheerful, your joy will bubble to the surface. Don't be surprised if you even burst into song!

Fun FacToid:

The word joy or some form of it (rejoice, enjoy, etc.) appears in the Bible 235 times!

Did You Know

. . . that joy and happiness mean different things? It's true. Happiness is temporary, but joy is constant—not affected by your circumstances.

More To Explore: Romans 15:13

Girl Talk:

Do you feel joyful most of the time? Would your friends consider you joyful, or maybe grouchy? Do you want more joy in your life?

God Talk:

"Lord, I want to be joyful, no matter what bad stuff comes my way. Please fill me with your never-ending joy so that others will be drawn to that joy in me. I love you, Lord. Amen."

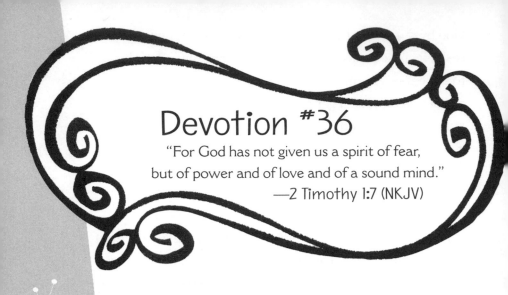

Devotion #36

"For God has not given us a spirit of fear,
but of power and of love and of a sound mind."
—2 Timothy 1:7 (NKJV)

What Are You Thinking?

It's common to fear trying new activities, going new places, making decisions, and giving a performance. But you don't have to be afraid! God hasn't given you that fear. Instead, he's given you courage and power for using your abilities, love, and good judgment. You can be level-headed, with your thoughts and feelings under control.

Maybe you study hard for a test, but you're still afraid you'll forget the answers. Or you must decide whether to go to a party, and you're afraid to hurt someone's feelings. Maybe you have a singing gift, but you're afraid to try out for the girls' chorus. Your fearful feelings mushroom out of control—and make the decisions for you.

What can you do? The Bible says God has given you power and love and a mind under control. That means, if you continue to be ruled by fear, it is a choice you make. God's choice for you is to have power, love, and a self-disciplined mind.

So how do we get over this fear? "You should not be like cowering, fearful slaves. You should behave instead like God's very own children, adopted into his family—calling him 'Father, dear Father.'" (Romans 8:15–16 NLT)

Instead of shrinking back in fear, call on your Father for help. He wants to give you a sound mind. Ask him for that, then step out in faith. Take that test. Try out for that musical. Enjoy living a life free from fear.

Self-control is a fruit of the Spirit. And that includes controlling your mind.

Did You Know

. . . the human brain has about 100,000,000,000 neurons? That's 100 billion!

More To Explore: Psalm 34:4-8

GirL TaLk:

Do you feel you make decisions confidently or out of fear of something else? Have you talked to God about it?

God TaLk:

"Lord, I am tired of making choices out of fear. Please help me rely on you and make confident choices. Thank you for being with me through every choice. Amen."

More Brain FacTs:

- The adult human brain is about two percent of the total body weight.
- The adult human brain weighs about three pounds.
- An elephant brain weighs over thirteen pounds.

Devotion #37

"Don't be concerned about the outward beauty that depends on fancy hairstyles, expensive jewelry, or beautiful clothes. You should be known for the beauty that comes from within, the unfading beauty of a gentle and quiet spirit, which is so precious to God."—I Peter 3:3–5 (NLT)

Unfading Beauty: An Inside Job

Do you want to have beauty that fades as you get older, or beauty that grows even stronger? For enduring beauty, don't depend on current hairstyles, costly jewelry, or designer clothes. The beauty that lasts is hidden within you. A gentle, quiet, unruffled, peaceful spirit is beautiful and precious to God!

Our current culture places all its importance on outer beauty. Beauty is a billion dollar business, including plastic surgery, exercise equipment, and designer clothing. From the movies to magazines, our world screams that outer beauty is all that matters. Not true! We all know girls who are gorgeous, but when they open their mouths, nasty things spew out. Suddenly they lose their beauty. If you're unhappy, lonely, insecure, and crabby, a total body make-over won't change a thing.

The beauty has to start in your heart.

How do you acquire this kind of beauty that is so precious to God? By spending time alone with him. Talk to him. Read his Word. The neat thing about inner beauty is its ability to transform how you look on the outside. Some of the most beautiful women in history didn't have good facial features or fancy clothes. They had an inner peace and a loving spirit that radiated, making them beautiful on the outside as well.

Enjoy fixing your hair and wearing pretty clothes, but don't depend on them to make you beautiful. Instead, give yourself God's beauty treatment. Remember, it's an inside job.

Did You Know

. . . that Julia and her friends from *Sophie's World* are examples of girls with no inner beauty? Watch out, Faithgirlz! These girls can get nasty!

More To Explore: 1 Timothy 2:9–10

Girl Talk:

How much time do you spend looking in the mirror and trying to improve your outer beauty? How much time do you spend in God's Word, improving your inner beauty?

God Talk:

"Lord, I care too much about how I look on the outside. Please help me focus on my spirit, to make it more loving and peaceful. Thank you for being the perfect example to work toward. Amen."

Beauty 101:

For instant change to your hairstyle, switch your part or make it into a zigzag!

Devotion #38

"Some sat in darkness and deepest gloom, miserable prisoners in chains. They rebelled against the words of God, scorning the counsel of the Most High."
—Psalm 107:10–11 (NLT)

Afraid of The Dark

What a frightening picture! Prisoners in chains, sitting in terrible dread and depression. They decided to reject the words of God, his advice and guidance, and do what they pleased instead. The end result was miserable despair—a result they chose for themselves.

People who are afraid of the dark keep all the lights on so they feel safe. Would it make sense, if you're afraid of the dark, to turn *off* the lights at midnight, then sit in pitch blackness? Of course not, but that's what some people do. They invite darkness and misery into their lives by living in rebellion of God's Word. By rejecting godly advice and counsel, they become prisoners in chains. They are prisoners to hatred or an appetite out of control. If they have accepted Jesus as Savior, they'll still go to heaven. But they won't enjoy their days on earth much!

Are you now stuck with a problem that has you in despair? If so, don't hesitate another minute. Flip on that light switch. Go to God, confess, and let him help you burst those chains. "Then they cried out to the LORD in their trouble, and He saved them out of their distresses. He brought them out of darkness and the shadow of death, and broke their chains in pieces." (Psalm 107:13–14, NKJV)

Once you've turned the lights back on, choose to live according to God's Word. Welcome his advice and guidance. Walk in the light as he is in the light.

Did You Know

. . . light is mentioned in the Bible 66 times? A great verse is John 8:12 (NIV), "I am the light of the world. Whoever follows me will never walk in darkness, but will have the light of life."

More To Explore: Isaiah 9:2 and Matthew 4:16

Girl Talk:

Do you feel in the dark because of a problem that keeps bothering you? Confess it to God, and turn the light on!

God Talk:

"Lord, I am really struggling with _____. I confess to you that I don't want to do it again. Please set me free from this darkness. Thank for never leaving me. Amen."

Devotion #39

"A fool gives full vent to anger, but a wise person quietly holds it back."
—Proverbs 29:11 (NLT)

GeT GLad!

A fool is someone who lacks good judgment. When he gets mad, he says everything on his mind, dumping anger on everyone in his way. A person with good judgment and common sense sets limits on herself and keeps her words under control.

Every day you'll have to choose between getting mad and being glad. When your little sis spills milk in your lap, you can yell at her or choose to hold the words back. When the dog chews up your homework, you can erupt in screaming or hold it back. When your best friend sits with someone else on the bus, you can chew her out or hold it back. It's your choice. Sometimes we pretend we can't control our angry words. "You don't understand! He made me *soooo* mad!" You can't always prevent the angry feelings, but you CAN choose what to do about them.

If the anger is milder, like having your brother beat you to the TV set and choose his favorite cartoon to watch, you can simply close your mouth, take several very slow deep breaths, and count silently to ten while your anger cools. If your anger is hotter, like if you see the neighborhood bully trash your backpack, you might have to take stronger measures. Leave the area before you can spew out a string of nasty, hateful words. Go somewhere, pray for help, and talk to someone you trust if necessary. Then deal with the situation calmly.

In life, things happen to us that make us angry. Let the fools spew everything on their minds. YOU watch your words, and choose to be wise.

Did You Know

. . . counting slowly to ten when you're ready to explode really works? It helps you stop and think before reacting and distracts you from what's making you so angry.

More To Explore: Proverbs 12:16

Girl Talk:

Why do Christians need to control their anger? Do you control your anger or do you "lose it" often?

God Talk:

"God, help me to choose peace and gladness over strife and anger. Help me to think before reacting. Thank you. Amen."

"Don't Get Mad . . ."

You feel that anger rising up.
You're getting really mad.
You want to yell and scream and kick.
But don't get mad, get glad!
Choose to love, not attack.
Un-grit your teeth and grin.
Take some deep breaths—in and out.
And slowly count to ten!

Devotion #40

"No, dear brothers and sisters, I am still not all I should be, but I am focusing all my energies on this one thing: Forgetting the past and looking forward to what lies ahead."—Philippians 3:13 (NLT)

Bury The Past

Nobody's perfect, and Paul admits that. But he's not wasting any time on regrets and guilt over his past failures. He wisely concentrates all his attention and energy on making a total change in his priorities. He clings to what is truly valuable, both here on earth and for eternity.

You may have things you want to forget too. Maybe you totally blew your speech in reading class. Or you tripped in the bleachers and fell on top of a crush-worthy boy. Or maybe a memory that tortures you is more serious. Perhaps you let somebody down in a big way or—like the apostle Paul—you have really hurt someone.

We all make mistakes and do things we aren't proud of later. Even after we ask God's forgiveness, the guilty feeling can linger. But you can't change the past or control it in any way. Do keep the lessons you learned, but forget the incidents and the emotions attached to them. The best way to do that is to focus on your future, both here on earth and in heaven to come. Focus on growing in godly values, and forget other things—both past failures and past successes. Nothing on earth compares to knowing Jesus better and better each day.

Whatever happened before today—good or bad—is in the past. Concentrate your energy and thoughts on what lies ahead. You'll see improvement over past failures, but even more important, you'll look forward to the truly priceless victory over death and an eternity with Christ.

Did You Know

. . . our memory and highest levels of thought occur in something only a few millimeters thick? Seventy percent of our brain cells are in the cortex, the brain's thin outer layer.

More To Explore: Luke 9:62 and Acts 9:1–31

GirL TaLk:

Do you think about past mistakes and worry over them? Are you stuck in the past?

≡ God TaLk:

"Lord, help me to quit fretting about things in the past. I want to look to the future. I give my concerns to you right now, in Jesus' name. Amen."

"No Fret"
No fret.
No sweat.
No regret.
You bet!

Devotion #41

"You will know them by their fruits. Do men gather grapes from thornbushes or figs from thistles? Even so, every good tree bears good fruit, but a bad tree bears bad fruit."—Matthew 7:16–17 (NKJV)

Tasty Fruit

Jesus says we will be known by our fruits. Our actions mirror what's in our hearts. Every time we speak or act, we are revealing who we truly are. If you really love God and want to live for him, your fruit—or actions—will show it.

Do you know girls who go to church and youth group and act one way, but their behavior changes completely at school where they want to be popular and cool? Don't be a thornbush who tries to disguise herself as a fig tree. If you really love God, let your behavior—your fruit—show it, no matter where you are. Does that mean your behavior will be perfect? No. An apple tree might have terrific looking fruit, except for one or two wormy ones. But it *doesn't* have thorns at all.

You can't fool people, at least not for

long. Just as we recognize pear and orange trees by the fruit hanging there, people will know you by *your* fruits. If your actions are consistently kind and generous, you will be known for that good fruit. If you're a gossip and backbiter, it won't matter how nice your leaves and branches look. You'll still be known as that rotten, prickly fruit.

We all like to be fruit inspectors. But instead of worrying about someone else's fruit, examine your own. Let your roots go down deeply into the soil of God's love. Plant yourself firmly in God's Word every day. Become a good tree, attractive to others, bearing good fruit.

Did You Know

. . . that eating forbidden fruit was the first sin? Read more about Adam and Eve's fateful snack in Genesis 3.

More To Explore: James 3:12

Girl Talk:

What kind of tree or thornbush would you describe yourself as right now? What can you do to become a healthy, fruitful tree?

God Talk:

"Lord, I want to be the same person at church, school, and everywhere. Help me to bear good fruit by being the kind, generous girl you want me to be. Amen."

Beauty 101:

What kinds of fruit do you gather when you're hungry? Every girl needs five servings of fruit and vegetables a day to help her skin, hair, and body stay healthy.

Devotion #42

"Don't worry about anything; instead, pray about everything. Tell God what you need, and thank him for all he has done."—Philippians 4:6 (NLT)

ALL AND Nothing

Don't be worried, concerned, anxious, troubled, or uneasy about *anything*; instead, talk to God about *everything*. Tell God what you need—he wants you to—but don't forget to thank him for what he has already done for you. If you do, you will develop a grateful heart. You will also be reminded that God has taken care of you in the past, and it will be easier to leave your cares with him this time too. You will find dozens of opportunities to worry every day, if you choose to. You may have personal troubles: your upcoming test, a sick parent, someone mad at you at school. You may worry about the state of the world: tragedies seen on TV, or a parent overseas in the military. Just remember: every opportunity to worry is also a chance to involve God in the matter. Since he's all-powerful, what better person to be involved?

Worry about nothing. Pray about everything. Simple to understand? Yes. Easy to do all the time? No. But it can become a habit over time. Like learning any new habit, it takes more effort at first. But if you do this each time a worry invades your mind, it will soon be an automatic response. You'll turn immediately to God, give him the concern, and thank him for however he is going to work it out.

Worry about nothing. Pray about everything. You'll see amazing answers in your life, and you'll develop a close personal relationship with the Lord. What a fabulous trade!

Did You Know

. . . that Jesus said not to worry about tomorrow? See Matthew 6:34 for Jesus' reassurance.

More To Explore: Matthew 6:25

Girl Talk:

Is there something you worry about on a regular basis? Do you see why it doesn't help you to dwell on it?

God Talk:

"Lord, I know I shouldn't worry, but it comes back again and again. I want to give this issue to you and not think about it again. Thank you for giving me peace. Amen."

Devotion #43

"I command you—be strong and courageous!
Do not be afraid or discouraged.
For the LORD your God is with you wherever
you go."—Joshua 1:9 (NLT)

Fight Fear—and Win!

God requires and demands that we be strong and brave.
It's not just a suggestion! God expects you to show great
strength and power and to face fearful things without running
away. Do not give into defeat or lose hope. For God is with
you no matter where you go.

Fears come in all shapes and sizes. You may be afraid of
the water, but you are required to take swimming lessons
at school. You may be moving, and you're afraid to go
to the new school. You may live in an area where
tornadoes or hurricanes are frequent. You
may be afraid that you'll never have a close
friend who really, really cares about you.

God never commands us to do something that he won't give us the power to
do. You can count on that. If he tells you
to have courage, to be brave, then he will
give you the strength and power to do it.

The courage comes from trusting God, no matter what happens. It's normal to feel fear. Most of the great men of the Bible felt horrible fear at times. God simply says that when you feel the fear, don't run. Don't flinch from doing what is right. Step out, and God will meet you there. And when the challenge is over, you'll realize God was with you—walking you through it step by step—all the way. You will feel much less fear the next time you face that situation.

You CAN face scary things without losing hope or running away. God has a firm grip on you. He's all-powerful, and because of that, you have more strength inside you than you can imagine. Be brave!

Did You Know

. . . that FaithGirlz! ask God for help in being courageous? Sophie wants to help Kitty, so she asks God how to do it. Find out what she does in *Sophie's World.*

More To Explore: Isaiah 43:1–2 and Psalm 27:1

GirL TaLk:

Imagine something you want to do, but are scared to try. Can you see yourself doing it with God's help?

God TaLk:

"God, sometimes I feel really scared about _____. I know you are there with me all the time. Please help me to put my trust in you and leave my fear behind! Amen."

Devotion #44

"Greater love has no one than this, than to lay down one's life for his friends."—John 15:13 (NKJV)

Best Friends Forever

The greatest sacrifice of all time was Jesus' dying on the cross to make it possible for us to go to heaven. He himself did nothing wrong, yet he died so that we might live. Jesus said that his followers were to love each other in the same way—ready to make sacrifices.

You probably will never have a chance to sacrifice your life for a friend in some dangerous, life-or-death situation. You may never be called on to rescue a drowning person or hunt in a blizzard for a lost child. However, you can make other sacrifices for your friends. What can you give up? Time. Energy. Sometimes money. You can give a friend time to listen to her problems when you'd rather go shopping or watch TV. You can help when a friend is loaded down with work or needs assistance on a project. And you can pray for them. Proverbs 17:17 says, "A friend loves at all times." That's more than when it's just fun or convenient. So if you want to go to a movie, but your friend's dog just died and she's very upset, your sacrifice might mean skipping the movie and listening to her as she cries. You might want to work on your suntan on Saturday afternoon, so it would be a sacrifice to give that up and help your friend babysit her three little cousins. While few of us will ever be called on to give up our lives for a friend, we can daily think of others and make the sacrifices that we can.

Jesus laid down his life for you. There is no greater love than that. Share the love of Jesus with a friend today.

Did You Know

. . . Jesus called himself a shepherd? In John 10:11 (NIV), he says he is "the good shepherd who lays down his life for his sheep." We are those sheep! Read it all in John 10:6–16.

More To Explore: Romans 5:6–8

Girl Talk:

Have you ever sacrificed something for a friend? How did that make you feel? How did your friend feel?

God Talk:

"Lord, I thank you for giving up your life for me. Help me find ways to help my friends and family and to help with a willing heart. Thank you for your wonderful example. Amen."

Devotion #45

"Then He said to His disciples, 'The harvest truly is plentiful, but the laborers are few.'"—Matthew 9:37 (NKJV)

HeLp WanTed!

If a farmer's bumper crop of corn is ripe and the fields are full, he won't have a harvest to sell unless plenty of workers run the machinery and get the crop to market. Jesus called the hurting people he preached to a huge harvest, ready for picking. Many people needed a Savior, but few people were willing to teach others the good news.

Are there people in your neighborhood, among your relatives—even at home—who don't know Jesus? This includes those you really like and those you don't like. Every soul is precious to Christ—the meanest kid in your grade as well as the kindest one. Jesus said they are like scattered sheep without a Good Shepherd.

Telling people about Jesus often makes us uncomfortable. Will they put you down or think you're crazy? They might. But it's also possible they will consider you the best friend they've ever had for sharing this good news with them. Don't put it off. Talk to them now. Invite them to church. Give them a Bible. Jesus said the harvest is ready NOW. "Do you not say, 'There are still four months and then comes the harvest'? Behold, I say to you, lift up your eyes and look at the fields, for they are already white for harvest!" (John 4:35 NKJV).

Pray and ask God if there is someone today he wants you to speak to. Ask God to give that person a heart to listen and to give you boldness to share. Help *is* wanted—you!

Did You Know

. . . that the Word of God says that God called both Jeremiah and John the Baptist before they were ever born? God has jobs set aside for us to do even before we are born!

More To Explore: Luke 10:2 and Ephesians 2:10

GirL TaLk:

Is there someone in your class or family that you would like to talk to about Jesus? How do you think they would respond to you?

God TaLk:

"Lord, I know it's important to tell your good news. I want to be courageous and talk to _____ about you. Please help me to find the best way to tell them. Thank you. Amen."

Devotion #46

"Lazy hands make a man poor, but diligent hands bring wealth."—Proverbs 10:4 (NIV)

Keep On Keepin' On

Lazy people don't pay attention or take enough care to do a good job, and they are soon poor. Workers who are diligent are those who persist and don't quit. They pay attention to detail, so they do an excellent job, and they get rich.

A lazy babysitter won't wash dishes, leaves the house in a mess, forgets to bathe the children, and feeds them junk food. Why? It's easier. She'd rather lie on the couch and nap, but she won't keep her job long. She has what the Bible calls a "slack hand." What will be her eventual end? "Laziness casts one into a deep sleep, and an idle person will suffer hunger" (Proverbs 19:15).

Diligence is critical to be successful in anything, not just making money. You won't be physically fit if you only exercise once a week. You won't play the piano well if you only practice once a month. You won't earn an A in math class if you only do your assignments occasionally. To be successful, we must do the right things, sometimes for a long period of time. Anyone can discipline herself for a day or two, but diligence (keeping on keeping on) brings rewards. That might be riches, or an A in a class, or a fit body, or an outstanding piano recital.

Whatever job you have to do—whether it's shoveling snow for your dad or weeding the garden for a neighbor—take care to do a super job. You'll earn a reputation for being an excellent worker, and more job opportunities will open up for you. With enough diligence, one day you may even be rich!

Did You Know

. . . that Proverbs 6:6–11 says we can learn from the ant? Ants live in colonies and have specialized groups within them called castes. There is a queen, and there are male bees, which take care of the colony, raise the babies, and bring in food. All their lives, they work hard!

More To Explore: Proverbs 21:5

Girl Talk:

Do you work diligently in school, at home? What is one area of your life that you could work on being more diligent?

God Talk:

"Lord, I know you are always working. Help me to be diligent in all that I do. I want people to see you when they see me. Thank you. Amen."

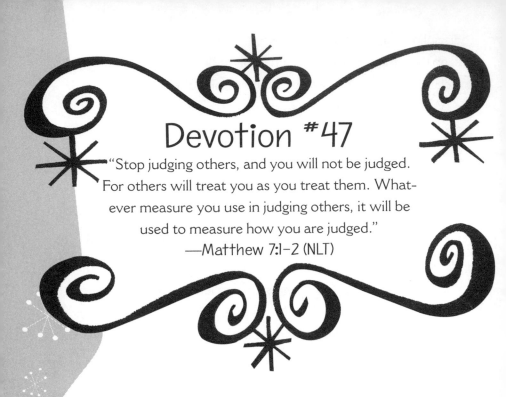

Devotion #47

"Stop judging others, and you will not be judged. For others will treat you as you treat them. Whatever measure you use in judging others, it will be used to measure how you are judged."
—Matthew 7:1-2 (NLT)

What Glasses Are You Wearing?

Stop forming negative opinions about other people, then people won't form negative opinions about you. Whatever standard you use to compare people will be the same standard others use to form an opinion of you.

It's almost instinctive to form opinions about others: their clothing and hair, the way they walk, how they talk, their grades, and their families. Judging is a pride issue. We judge someone as inferior so we can feel superior. Everything we observe gives us a chance to judge—or show mercy. If you're kind in your judgments of others, it's like wearing pink-tinted sunglasses that color everything rosy. Judging harshly is using a magnifying glass to focus on someone's faults to make them even bigger.

If you have a judging habit, catch yourself when you form a negative opinion about someone else's looks or actions. Then replace it with something positive, out loud, if possible. Your first reaction might be to think, "Marie walks like a duck." Counter that thought with, "How Marie walks is none of my business." Then, if you're with someone, say out loud, "I love the color of Marie's shoes." The more consistently you replace judgmental thoughts with positive ones, the quicker you'll break the habit.

No one likes to be judged. Choose to form positive opinions about people. Then watch how they'll look at *you* through rose-colored glasses.

Did You Know

. . . that the book of Judges is a collection of accounts of the lives of "judges"? They ruled Israel during the 300 years between the death of Joshua and before the reign of Israel's first king, Saul.

More To Explore:

James 4:11–12 and Luke 6:37

Girl Talk:

Do you have a habit of judging others? Would you rather be looked at under a microscope or through rose-colored glasses?

God Talk:

"God, I am so thankful that you are a merciful judge. Help me to see the positive in others as you see the positive in me.

Thank you. Amen."

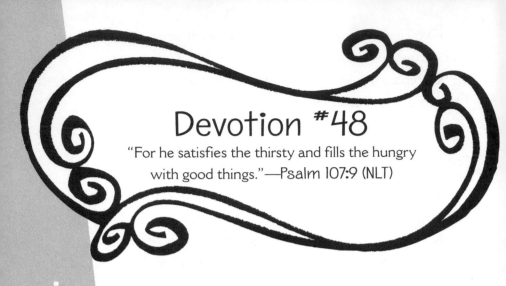

Devotion #48

"For he satisfies the thirsty and fills the hungry with good things."—Psalm 107:9 (NLT)

How Hungry Are You?

God satisfies our spirit like good food fills our bodies. God fills us up and meets our needs. He quenches our thirst and satisfies our hunger with excellent and desirable things.

You get hungry every day. Would your body be happy with one meal per week? Not! In fact, many people eat much more than three times a day to feel satisfied. One meal per week would eventually kill you. Your spirit needs feeding too, and the Bible contains our spiritual food. Sitting in church for one hour per week feeds your soul as much as one meal per week would feed your body. Major anorexia! You can become depressed, anxious, fearful, critical, and impatient—all signs of a starving and malnourished soul.

Set aside some time to be quiet with God every day. Start out small, if this is new to you. Five or ten minutes of Bible reading, plus five or ten minutes of prayer is fine to start. Making it a habit is your first goal. Your soul may be starving, but small daily meals of the Word will bring it back to full health.

Suppose you just don't feel hungry for God's Word. Most days you don't even think of reading your Bible or praying. Then pray and ask God to increase your spiritual hunger and thirst. He delights to answer prayers like that! When we're hungry and thirsty enough, we'll go to the source of our food and eat till full. "Those who seek the LORD shall not lack any good thing." (Psalm 34:10 NIV)

So dig into God's Word first thing every morning, and eat your fill. It satisfies!

Did You Know

. . . that Jesus refers to the Holy Spirit as "living water"? If you have this living water, you will never be thirsty spiritually again! See more in John 7:37–39.

More To Explore: John 6:35 and Matthew 5:6

Girl Talk:

Do you have that spiritual hunger for God's Word? Do you want to be filled by God?

God Talk:

"Thank you, Lord, for giving me food to sustain my physical body. Please increase my spiritual appetite, so that I may grow closer to you. Help me to make time for your Word in my life. Amen."

Beauty 101:

Try to stick to milk and water to quench your thirst. Sodas are a treat—once a week is plenty, and fewer soft drinks will keep your teeth pearly white!

Devotion #49

"I assure you, even if you had faith as small as a mustard seed you could say to this mountain, 'Move from here to there,' and it would move. Nothing would be impossible."—Matthew 17:20 (NLT)

Mountain-Moving Faith

Jesus promises that you can do mighty things, even if your trust in him is as tiny as a mustard seed—smaller than an ant! You can say to some problem that appears huge, 'Move from here to there,' and it will move. Jesus said there is nothing that can't be accomplished or handled. Nothing!

Do you have a mountain in your life, one that is an obstacle to you? A mountain of family problems, or money problems? Maybe it's how you feel about your physical appearance. Maybe it's your difficulty studying and remembering your school work. God is in the mountain-moving business. Our part is to believe—to have faith—that he can do it. When you trust, sometimes he suddenly takes care of the problem for you; he may remove a person from your life or give you an after-school job out of the blue. Or he sends a person to help you who knows just what to do. Often God personally shows you, step by step, the things you can do to solve the problem. They're usually things you had never considered—and wouldn't have thought of on your own. "What is impossible with men is possible with God." (Luke 18:27 NIV)

The most important thing in receiving God's help is not our faith (which can be small), but his great faithfulness to keep his Word. We don't need self-confidence, but we need God-confidence.

Do you want greater faith? Faith is like a muscle. It only gets stronger by using it. Put your faith in God today, and watch that mountain start to move!

Did You Know

. . . that a mustard seed is as small as a poppy seed and grows into a tall tree? Jesus says the tree is like the kingdom of heaven. Read what he says about it in Matthew 13:31–32.

More To Explore: Mark 9:23

Girl Talk:

Do you believe God can move mountains? Do you have a mountain that needs moving?

God Talk:

"Lord, I want to have mountain-moving faith. Help me to trust in you at all times. I know you are always willing to help me. Thank you Lord. Amen."

Fun Factoid:

Mount Everest is the highest mountain in the world at 29,035 feet. That's five and a half miles high!

Devotion #50

"'Come, follow me,' Jesus said, 'and I will make you fishers of men.'"—Matthew 4:19 (NIV)

Go Fish!

When Jesus started his preaching ministry, he began to gather followers. These people (disciples) would first hear his teaching. Then afterwards they could teach and preach to others, telling about the things they had seen Jesus do. Jesus still calls us to follow him and learn from him, and then lead others to Christ.

You know many people—at school, in your neighborhood, maybe even in your own home—who don't know Jesus as their Savior. How can you introduce these people to Jesus?

"Let your light shine before men in such a way that they may see your good works, and glorify your Father who is in heaven." (Matthew 5:16 NASB)

In other words, let your good efforts shine out in such a way that others will know your faith in God is real. Letting your light shine can be as simple as putting a smile on your face, saying a kind word to someone, or giving a sincere compliment. How you *live* is just as important as what you *say* to others about Jesus. It's like the bait when you go fishing—it's attractive and makes people come closer.

Maybe you've heard this called "witnessing." Often we fear we'll do a poor job in telling others about Christ. Remember: it doesn't depend on you. Jesus shows us how. First, he says, "Follow me." Spend time with him, talk to him, get to know him. Then he says that *he* will make us able to witness effectively with our mouths and our lives and actions.

So grab your bait and pole—and go fishing!

Did You Know

. . . that Jesus' disciples gave up everything to follow him? They left their jobs, families, and homes all because he said, "Follow me!" Wow! See Luke 18:28–30.

More To Explore: Luke 5:10–11.

Girl Talk:

What can you do today to "let your light shine"? Do you have someone in mind to talk to about Jesus?

God Talk:

"Father, I want to lead others to you, but I'm afraid. Please give me courage and strength to do what you want me to do. Please prepare their hearts to understand. Amen."

Fun Factoid:

More than ninety percent of all fish caught are captured in the northern hemisphere. Fish are caught to be eaten or to make things like glue, soap, and fertilizer.

Devotion #51

"God, who gives life to the dead and calls into being that which does not exist."—Romans 4:17 (NASB)

Get Your Faith Eyes in Focus

God does miracles. Many times in the New Testament, Jesus brings a dead person back to life. Jesus himself rose from the dead. God also creates something out of nothing, bringing into existence what didn't exist before, like when he created the heavens and the earth. When he said, "Let there be light," the sun, moon, and stars were formed.

God can call things into existence for you too. What do you need that you don't have right now? A best friend? A new flute to replace a broken one? What things would you like to have? A place on the track team? A new dress that's not in your budget? Pray and ask God for what you need. Philippians 4:19 promises that God will supply everything you need (but not necessarily everything you *want*). God knows what would be the best for you in every situation. He often gives us something even better, if we're patient and leave the choice to him.

Use your God-given imagination for seeing

the good things God can do in your life instead of the bad things you fear might happen. This is not a magic potion or using mind control to get what you want. For God to make something happen, it must be his will for your life.

What you imagine affects what you do. If you imagine yourself stumbling and falling in a race, you are much more likely to do that. If you focus on running swiftly and sure-footed, you are more likely to succeed. Your thinking determines your feelings about situations, and your feelings determine your actions.

Use your God-given imagination to see yourself as God sees you!

Did You Know

. . . that at least 50 years before it happened, Noah believed a flood would occur because God had promised it? Read Genesis 6:9–22.

More To Explore: Luke 7:11–16

Girl Talk:

Do you spend a lot of time thinking about things you don't have? Have you tried asking God what he wants for you?

God Talk:

"Lord, I know you want what is best for me. Please help me to ask for what you want, not what I want. Thank you for loving me. Amen."

Mini-Quiz:

1. God promised Moses _____ in Exodus 3:18.
2. God promised to give Solomon _____ in 1 Kings 3.

Answers: 1. success 2. wisdom

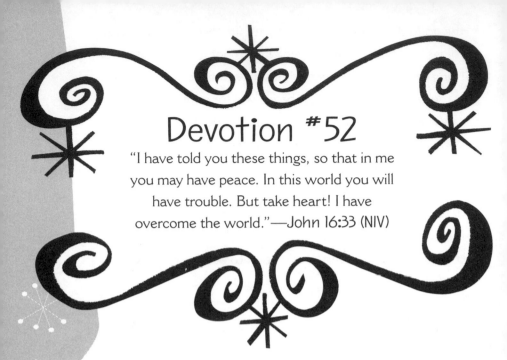

Devotion #52

"I have told you these things, so that in me you may have peace. In this world you will have trouble. But take heart! I have overcome the world."—John 16:33 (NIV)

Nothing Is Too Big for God

Jesus wants you to have a life full of peace, but he knew you'd also have some troubles and sorrows. Cheer up! That doesn't have to steal your peace. Take heart and have courage. As children of God, we are "in Christ." Since Jesus has defeated and overcome the world, that makes us conquerors too!

Are you facing trouble right now? Trouble with a bully? Trouble with your family? You see no way out. The Israelites felt the same way when the armies of Egypt chased them and the Red Sea blocked their escape route. They cried out to their leader, Moses, saying "What have you done to us by bringing us out of Egypt?" Moses replied, "Do not be afraid. Stand firm and you will see the deliverance the Lord will bring you today . . . The Lord will fight for you; you need only to be still." God parted the

Red Sea. The Israelites walked through on dry ground, and the sea closed again to swallow up the Egyptian armies (Exodus 14).

Like the Israelites, if you've accepted Jesus as your Savior, you're one of God's chosen people. He'll help you overcome your problem too—and totally defeat it. When facing a difficult situation, ask God to make a way through it for you. He will. You may have to step out and do something scary, just as the Israelites did when walking between high walls of water on each side.

Cheer up! No matter what your trouble, "in all these things we are more than conquerors through him who loved us." (Romans 8:37 NIV)

Did You Know

. . . that an angel helped Paul escape from prison, while many soldiers guarded him? God delivered! Read Acts 12:5–11 for the full story.

More To Explore: Exodus 14

Girl Talk:

Have you ever had a situation where you felt there was no way out? How did you deal with it?

God Talk:

"Lord, I'm really scared about _____. Please help me get through this. I want to be courageous for you. Amen."

Fun Factoid:

In 1978, numerous chariot parts were found in the Red Sea. A later dive found an eight-spoke wheel only used during Ramses II's and Tutmoses' reign. (Ramses was pharaoh at the time of the Israelites' exodus.)

Devotion #53

"He is like a man building a house, who dug down deep and laid the foundation on rock. When a flood came, the torrent struck that house but could not shake it, because it was well built."—Luke 6:48 (NIV)

How's Your Foundation?

Some days, it seems like everything in our lives is on shaky ground. Take courage in the fact that God's Word, the foundation on which he stands, is firm and solid. It never moves or changes. The Lord knows who belong to him. That's *you*, if you've accepted Jesus as your Savior.

A firm foundation is critical when building things. Suppose you're helping your brother build a toy house with blocks. Without a broad base at the bottom, the blocks on top soon topple over. Or when cheerleading teams build pyramids, the strongest members make up the bottom row. Then the lighter weight members will be safely held up. When a new house is built, cement provides a solid foundation. When a storm comes, the house will still be standing after the storm passes. You want the same kind of solid foundation in your own life. How do you acquire it? By studying God's Word, then applying it to the situations in your life. If you do that on a consistent basis, you can avoid many of the storms by wise actions. If you don't bother, "you ignored my advice and rejected the correction I offered," then "calamity overcomes you like a storm, you are engulfed by trouble, and anguish and distress overwhelm you." (Proverbs 1:25, 27 NLT) What a horrible price to pay for rebellion!

Some storms come into every girl's life though, even when you do everything right. When they come, make sure there aren't any leaks in your foundation, then ride out the storm. When it's over, you'll still be standing!

Did You Know

. . . two Faithgirlz! go through an almost impossible situation at school in *Sophie's World*? How does God deliver them? Read to find out more!

More To Explore: 2 Timothy 2:1

Girl Talk:

Are you facing serious problems in your life today? Does your foundation ever feel ready to collapse?

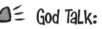

God Talk:

"Lord, I don't want a flimsy foundation. I want to build my foundation upon your Word. Please help me to do that Lord. I love you. Amen."

Devotion #54

"So we don't look at the troubles we can see right now; rather, we look forward to what we have not yet seen. For the troubles we see will soon be over, but the joys to come will last forever."
—2 Corinthians 4:18 (NLT)

Joy Forever

What you look at and focus on will determine your level of joy. So don't look at the troubles you're facing now. Take your eyes off them. Instead, look forward to what you'll inherit in heaven. It doesn't seem like it now, but your troubles will pass. The joy of life in God's presence, where there will be no more tears or pain, will last forever.

Everything in this world is temporary, both the things you love and the things you hate. Problems with your parents and at school will pass away. It's the same for the good things: your solo in band, your cool wardrobe, and that new mountain bike. Even the things we like are temporary, but heaven will provide such fabulous attractions that these good earthly things will hardly seem worth noticing.

If you've accepted Jesus as your Savior, your real home is already reserved for you in heaven. How should you live on earth now? "So we are always confident, even though we know that as long as we live in these bodies we are not at home with the LORD. That is why we live by believing and not by seeing" (2 Corinthians 5:6-7). In other words, we walk by faith in our heavenly future, and not by sight. It's not easy. It takes self-discipline to choose our thoughts and focus on God.

Try it. You'll like it! Fill your mind with the joy to come that will last forever.

Did You Know

. . . that the apostle Paul survived many trials in his life? He was whipped, shipwrecked, and chased by angry mobs, yet he called these trials "light and momentary." Read 2 Corinthians 4:16–18.

More To Explore: Romans 8:24–25 and Hebrews 11:1

Girl Talk:

Are you relying on God's will, not your own, for your decisions? Is it hard to go by faith instead of what you can actually see?

God Talk:

"Lord, it's easier to do what I want and not wait for you. Help me to wait for your answers and to faithfully do what you want. Thank you for always being there for me. Amen."

Devotion #55

"I suggest that you finish what you started a year ago, for you were the first to propose this idea, and you were the first to begin doing something about it. Now you should carry this project through to completion just as enthusiastically as you began it."
—2 Corinthians 8:10-11 (NLT)

Crossing The Finish Line

When you begin a project, don't quit halfway through. Stir up your original enthusiasm, and complete the project.

Do you have unfinished papers for school, chores at home, or craft projects? Did you make a promise—like visiting a nursing home weekly—but you haven't gone in a month? Good beginnings are great, but if you don't complete it, you won't gain any benefit. Neither will anyone else. Excuses like these don't count: "I meant to do that last weekend, but I got invited to the mall."

We begin projects with enthusiasm and a rush of emotions. Someone wants our help, and we promise without thinking. Then, when the mood passes, we regret starting the projects. As our enthusiasm dies, the unfinished projects collect dust.

How can you prevent having unfinished projects? "But don't begin until you count the cost. For who would begin construction of a building without first getting estimates and then checking to see if there is enough money to pay the bills? Otherwise, you might complete only the foundation before running out of funds." (Luke 14:28–30 NLT) Do you have enough time, money, and energy to complete the project? If not, wait for a better time.

Think carefully before saying you'll do something. Then be a person whose word is true, someone who can be counted on. Finish what you start.

Did You Know

. . . that Joshua, who followed Moses as leader of the Israelites, had a big responsibility when he started his job? He was supposed to lead the people into Canaan and go to battle. He leaned on God—you should too! See Joshua 1:1–11.

More To Explore: Romans 5:3–4

Girl Talk:

Do you have unfinished projects? What should you do if you are asked to take on another project?

God Talk:

"Lord, please help me complete what I've started. Help me to talk with you first, before beginning anything else. Thank you for giving me strength and advice. I love you. Amen."

Devotion #56

"Then Peter came to Jesus and asked, 'Lord, how many times shall I forgive my brother when he sins against me? Up to seven times?' Jesus answered, 'I tell you, not seven times, but seventy-seven times.'"
—Matthew 18: 21–22 (NIV)

Forgive How Many Times?

Peter shows what we all feel at times. While we love the mercy and forgiveness God gives us on a daily basis, we resent having to forgive other people, especially when they do the same thing over and over. Does Jesus mean we have to forgive seventy-seven times—and then we can clobber the offender? No, he's making a point: we need to forgive over and over, just as God forgives us daily. Forgiveness is a gift given to those who don't deserve it.

Every day, people do things that hurt us. Most do it by accident. Your forgetful grandmother thought your birthday was next month and missed it today. Your best friend has to cancel your movie date to do her homework. Some people, however, hurt others on purpose. Friends who make fun of you, but say they're "just teasing," know what they're doing. Forgive them, but ask them to stop. If they don't, find new friends. Being forgiving isn't the same as putting up with continual meanness.

Galatians 6:2 (AMP) says we need to "bear (endure, carry) one another's burdens and troublesome moral faults." It's easier to endure other people's faults when we realize how many we have ourselves. Instead of becoming bitter, "be gentle and forbearing with one another." (Colossians 3:13 AMP)

Give the gift of forgiveness to someone you know today.

Did You Know

. . . that forgiving is part of the Lord's Prayer? "And forgive us our debts, as we also have forgiven our debtors." (Matthew 6:9–13 NASB) Some versions say " . . . our trespasses, as we forgive those who trespass against us."

More To Explore: Luke 17:3–4

Girl Talk:

Have you been hurt by someone you care about? How are you dealing with it? Have you forgiven that person?

God Talk:

"Thank you for forgiving all my sins, Lord. Help me to be a forgiving person, too. Please take away the hurt I feel inside. I want to start over. Thank you for always being with me. Amen."

Devotion #57

"A cheerful heart is good medicine, but a broken spirit saps a person's strength."—Proverbs 17:22 (NLT)

Laughter, The Best Medicine

Modern doctors are now learning what the Bible has known all along. A lively, high-spirited, joyful heart is good for your health, just like medicine. Laughter can lessen the symptoms of certain diseases and strengthen your immune system. By contrast, a subdued, weakened spirit drains a person's strength, leaving him exhausted and weak. Believe it or not, the choice is yours!

When you receive bad news—a poor grade on a test, your friend is moving—you have two choices. You can cry and get depressed and eat a box of chocolates. Or you can smile, choose cheerful uplifting words to share, and help transform a bad situation into a hopeful one.

Being cheerful is a choice. Most of us have known people who didn't have much to be cheerful about, but chose to be upbeat and happy anyway. They've learned a great secret. They know being cheerful will help keep them strong.

As one preacher put it, "If you have the joy of the Lord, notify your face." In other words, smile! Proverbs 15:13 says a joyful, glad heart should produce a cheerful, happy face. Stand in front of the mirror, crack a big smile, and feel the immediate inner change. Focus on the fact that the all-powerful God of the universe is your Father and has everything under control. Choosing to be cheerful, no matter what the circumstances, will make you strong. "Do not sorrow, for the joy of the LORD is your strength" (Nehemiah 8:10 NKJV).

Go on. Smile. Take your medicine. It tastes great!

Did You Know

. . . that laughing 100 times is equal to ten minutes on the rowing machine or fifteen minutes on an exercise bike? Laughing could be your work-out plan!

More To Explore:
Proverbs 15:30 and Psalm 126:2–3

Girl Talk:

Have you ever wanted to gripe about something but said something positive instead? How does that make you feel?

God Talk:

"Lord, I know things can't always go my way. Help me to smile in all things and look to you for comfort and relief. Thank you for always being here with me. Amen."

Fun Factoid:

Can you believe it? Five hundred professors and other professionals belong to the International Society for Humor Studies. They take laughter pretty seriously!

Devotion #58

"'My thoughts are completely different from yours,' says the LORD. 'And my ways are far beyond anything you could imagine. For just as the heavens are higher than the earth, so are my ways higher than your ways and my thoughts higher than your thoughts.'"—Isaiah 55:8–9 (NKJV)

Heavenly Thoughts

Man will never completely understand God because he thinks and acts beyond anything we can imagine in our limited, human minds. God and man see things and people so differently. Just as heaven is beyond our understanding, God's ways are higher in quality than ours.

For example, you may have difficulty forgiving people, and you still remember what they did to you. God, on the other hand, forgives and forgets, removing your sin far from you (Psalm 103:12). Sometimes we consider ourselves very "spiritual" when we manage not yelling at someone. However, God says our thoughts must be right too, and that hating someone is like murder in our hearts (Matthew 5:21–22).

God's thoughts about events in your life are different than yours too. You might pray to remain in your home town, but your dad gets transferred to another state anyway.

Why? We don't know, but if you prayed about it, and the result is something you still don't want, remember that God's thoughts and ways are far superior to yours. He knows the beginning of your life, the middle "now" part, and the future. He knows where the blessings for you lie—and it may be living in a *new* town.

Strive to know God better through prayer and Bible study, but know that you'll never totally understand him or his ways. That's okay. That's why he's God!

Did You Know

. . . the Bible promises God will never leave us? Deuteronomy 31:8 (MSG) says, "God is striding ahead of you. He's right there with you. He won't let you down; he won't leave you. Don't be intimidated. Don't worry."

More To Explore: Psalm 92:5 and Romans 11:33–35

Girl Talk:

Are you facing a difficult situation right now? Are you blaming God for it, or do you trust him to see you through it?

God Talk:

"Thank you, Lord, for everything you do for me. Please help me make it through this difficult situation. I know that you know what is best for me. Please help me to see it too. Amen."

Devotion #59

"Now there are different kinds of spiritual gifts, but it is the same Holy Spirit who is the source of them all. There are different kinds of service in the church, but it is the same Lord we are serving. There are different ways God works in our lives, but it is the same God who does the work through all of us."—I Corinthians 12:4-6 (NLT)

No Cookie-Cutter Christians

Believers are not cut out with cookie cutters. God made us individuals, with different gifts to share with one another. Although our gifts are different, they all come from one source: the Holy Spirit. God works in our lives very differently, but it is still the same God working in each of us.

Are you afraid to use a gift or talent because it doesn't seem very important? Have you refused to use your talent because someone else can do it better? Or are you very talented, giving solos and doing "important" jobs at school or church? Do you secretly think your talent is better than someone else's?

Not everyone is a performer, nor wants to be. Does that mean you have no gifts? Not at all! "God has given each of us the ability to do certain things well . . . If your gift is that of serving others, serve them well . . . If your gift is to encourage others, do it! If you have money, share it generously . . . And if you have a gift for showing kindness to others, do it gladly" (Romans 12:6–8 NLT). Serving, sharing, encouraging, showing kindness—these are things we can all do.

You are unique. Share your unique gifts, and watch God use you to be a blessing to others.

Did You Know

. . . that your talents were given to you to share? "God has given gifts to each of you from his great variety of spiritual gifts. Manage them well so that God's generosity can flow through you." (1 Peter 4:10 NLT)

More To Explore: 1 Corinthians 12:7–11

Girl Talk:

Think of a few talents you have. Are you hiding them or using them? Are you using them to be in the spotlight or for God's purpose?

God Talk:

"Lord, I know you have given me many talents. Help me to realize what they are and to use them for your glory. Thank you for giving so much to me. Amen."

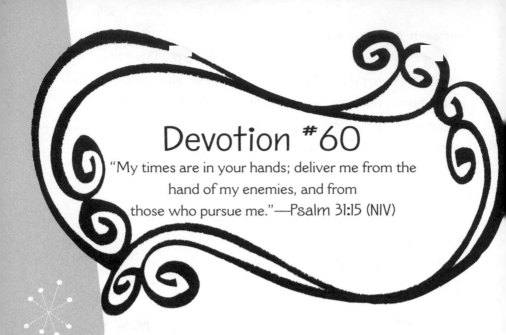

Devotion #60

"My times are in your hands; deliver me from the hand of my enemies, and from those who pursue me."—Psalm 31:15 (NIV)

Pick On Somebody Your Own Size!

When David wrote this psalm, he was being hunted down by a king who wanted him dead. David knew that his future was in God's powerful hand, and he prayed to be rescued from his enemies who had caused him great suffering.

Perhaps you feel hunted down some days too. Is there a bully on the bus who takes your lunch money? Or someone in your home who pushes you around or calls you names? If you are being bullied, *first* report it and get yourself away from that person. Don't stand and take it, thinking a "good Christian" shouldn't mind. God's will for your life is not abuse!

But when you're safe, there is more to be done if you want to handle bullies God's way. You will be tempted to do something for revenge to "get the bully back." Don't! Romans 12:19–21 (NLT) says, "Dear friends, never avenge yourselves. Leave that to God. For it is written, 'I will take vengeance; I will repay those who deserve it,' says the LORD. Instead, do what the Scriptures say: 'If your enemies are hungry, feed them. If they are thirsty, give them something to drink, and they will be ashamed of what they have done to you. Don't let evil get the best of you, but conquer evil by doing good.'" Is this easy? NO! But it works. Deal with bullies God's way, and he will take care of you. He may change the bully or remove the bully from your life.

Put your trust in God. He will deliver you.

Did You Know

. . . that girls' daily exposure to bullying rose 88 percent from 2001 to 2002, according to the National Crime Prevention Council?

More To Explore: Ephesians 6:13

Girl Talk:

Have you ever encountered a bully? If so, how did you react? Were you afraid?

God Talk:

"Lord, thank you for taking care of me. When bullies threaten me, please help me to stay calm and be kind. I want to be the person you want me to be. Amen."

Mini-Quiz:

If a bully bothers you (T/F) . . .

1. say firmly, "Leave me alone!" and walk away.
2. keep the incident to yourself.
3. join other people.

answers: 1. T 2. F–tell an adult! 3. T–being alone attracts bullies

Devotion #61

"But I tell you who hear me: Love your enemies, do good to those who hate you, bless those who curse you, pray for those who mistreat you."—Luke 6:27-28 (NIV)

You Want Me To Do What?

Jesus has a plan for dealing with our enemies, if we are willing to listen. He says to love them, do good things for them, and pray for their happiness. So pray for these things. Loving them includes being patient and kind, not being jealous or rude.

Pray for the teacher who ridiculed you? Horrible idea! Do good things for the person who enjoys being mean to you? Never! Why would Jesus ask us to do such things? For one reason, it releases God's power into that person's life. He can bring about circumstances to encourage that enemy to be willing to seek God. The other reason to love your enemies is that it releases God's power to work in *your* life. It is nearly impossible to be bitter and resentful about someone you pray for. And God knows *you* will be the one who suffers most if a root of bitterness grows in your heart.

Some things we do out of obedience to God, whether we want to or not. Praying for and loving our enemies is one of those things—at least at first. It will be the last thing you want to do. But once you start, if you keep it up when that person comes to mind, your hurt feelings will heal. You'll truly want God to work in their life.

Loving and praying for your enemy will work wonders in your own heart. It may even turn that enemy into a friend.

Did You Know

. . . that Christian love "keeps no record of wrongs" and "does not delight in evil"? It's true! The famous chapter about love, 1 Corinthians 13, tells us about love.

Girl Talk:

Have you ever prayed for someone who was mean to you? Have you seen any change in them or yourself?

God Talk:

"Lord, I know I should pray for those who are mean to me, but it is very hard. Please help me to pray for everyone I know, those I love and those I am trying to love. Thank you. Amen."

More To Explore . . . Luke 6:35–36, Proverbs 24:17; 25:21–22

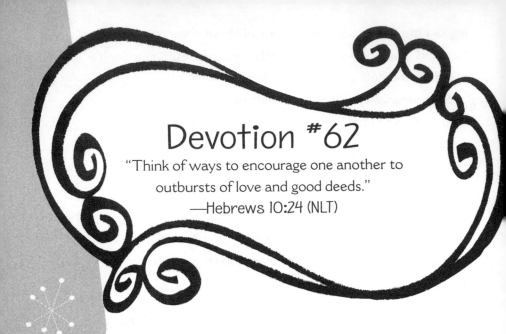

Devotion #62

"Think of ways to encourage one another to outbursts of love and good deeds."
—Hebrews 10:24 (NLT)

Be a Spirit Lifter

To encourage means to inspire someone with courage and hope, to raise their confidence and lift their spirits. It means to think of ways to contribute to someone else's growth or progress. We are to spur each other on to perform good efforts and generous expressions of love. Believers are to think about how they can be of service to others.

Do you know anyone who needs some encouragement? Do you have a friend whose family is going through a divorce? A sister who didn't make the cut on the basketball team? How could you convince your friends or family members to be of service (along with you) to build up this person's spirits?

Could you have a sleepover for your friend, where you do activities she would enjoy? Maybe your family could have a "Happy UNbirthday" party to cheer up your sister. Don't just feel sorry for someone. Instead, do something positive. "Dear children, let us stop just saying we love each other; let us really show it by our actions." (1 John 3:18–19 NLT) Right now, you might be thinking, "But who's going to encourage *me*?" Unfortunately, many believers feel like they can't help someone else if they're feeling down in the dumps themselves. Not true!

In fact, that's one of the nice things about lifting someone else's spirits. While you are busy encouraging people and getting your friends to help, your *own* joy will go through the roof!

Did You Know

. . . Paul wrote a beautiful prayer to the church. Part of it is: "May the LORD make your love increase and overflow for each other and for everyone else, just as ours does for you." (1 Thessalonians 3:12 NIV)

More To Explore . . . Galatians 5:13–15

GirL TaLk:

Do you know someone who could use some encouragement? How could you help them?

God TaLk:

"Lord, I want to help others. Help me to find ways to encourage others and give them joy. I want to be like you. Thank you. Amen."

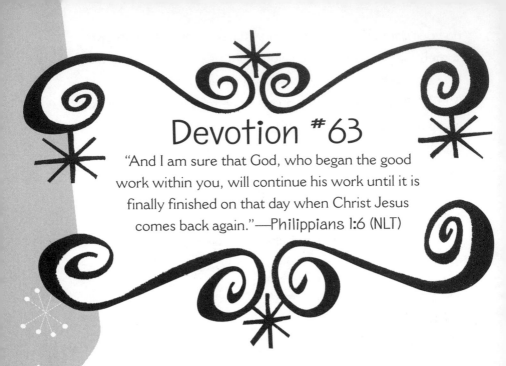

Devotion #63

"And I am sure that God, who began the good work within you, will continue his work until it is finally finished on that day when Christ Jesus comes back again."—Philippians 1:6 (NLT)

Under Construction

God is the master builder, in charge of constructing your life. He began his good work in you, and he will keep building your life until it is finally finished. When will that be? On the day Jesus returns. Ephesians 2:10 says "we are God's workmanship" or "masterpiece."

Masterpiece, huh? What about the days you're a rotten friend, a mouthy daughter, an insensitive sister? Are you still God's workmanship? Yes, without a doubt. While you live on this earth, you'll be under God's construction every day. He's building a great work of art in your life, but many days you won't look, act, or feel like a masterpiece. It takes time. Like the buildings you see go up, the beautiful and sturdy ones aren't built in a day or a week or a month. Some days they don't look like a masterpiece under construction. Rough boards instead of tile floors and planks instead of marble stairs—no one would guess how beautiful the finished work will be.

Your life is like that. Each of us is a "work in progress." Some days we look more like a masterpiece than others. God loves us just as much on the days we mess up as the days we shine for him. He knows our life is a learning process—and he sees the finished masterpiece he has in mind.

Did You Know

. . . that Noah and Solomon worked on masterpieces for God? Noah built the ark, and Solomon built the temple, where the ark of the covenant was kept.

More To Explore:
Philippians 1:9–11 and 3:13–14

Girl Talk:

Do you feel like you are under construction? Can you see God working in your life?

God Talk:

"Lord, thank you for never giving up on me. I want to keep working toward being a masterpiece for you. I love you. Amen."

Fun Factoid:

Many priceless treasures were made for the temple by Solomon's best woodworkers and craftsmen. Items made included two bronze pillars, 27 feet high, and a golden altar. To see the whole jaw-dropping list, read 1 Kings 7.

Devotion #64

"A tiny rudder makes a huge ship turn wherever the pilot wants it to go, even though the winds are strong. So also, the tongue is a small thing, but what enormous damage it can do. A tiny spark can set a great forest on fire."
—James 3:4–5 (NLT)

Only You Can Prevent Forest Fires

A small child can steer a huge horse because the tiny bit in the horse's mouth pinches and presses, forcing the horse to turn or stop. A pilot can turn a huge ship because a small vertical plate is attached under water at the rear of the ship. Your tongue is a very small thing too, but it also has vast power. Smokey the Bear warns us not to drop matches because a tiny spark could start a forest fire. Your tongue is like that match and can do enormous damage.

Have you ever had a classmate call you "clumsy," or a teacher remark that you're "slow"? Name calling hurts, sometimes so badly you can barely breathe. The words can go deep down into your heart. There they sit. And fester. And nibble at your self-esteem. You might even come to believe the words. So you quit ballet—which you love—because you were called clumsy. You stop trying to learn new things—after all, you're "slow."

You know how much words can wound you, so tame your own tongue so you don't damage others. Words have a way of replaying in our minds, over and over, day after day and year after year.

"The tongue has the power of life and death." (Proverbs 18:21 NIV) Be determined that you will use *your* power to love and encourage others.

Did You Know

. . . that you speak what is in your heart, even if you say you didn't mean it? "For whatever is in your heart determines what you say." (Matthew 12:34 NLT)

More To Explore: Proverbs 12:18; Proverbs 15:2

Girl Talk:

Have you felt wounded by words, or have you wounded others? How did you feel?

God Talk:

"Lord, my tongue is hard to control. I want to use it to encourage and love, instead of hurting others. Thank you for always caring. Amen."

Beauty 101:

Try this trick for better breath. Boil two cups of water, add a couple broken cinnamon sticks and simmer for five minutes. Cool, strain the liquid, and keep in water bottle for a natural mouthwash.

Devotion #65

"But I am like an olive tree flourishing in the house of God; I trust in God's unfailing love for ever and ever."—Psalm 52:8 (NIV)

Love for a Lifetime

Believers are like healthy trees that grow strong and are loaded down with good, juicy fruit. Believers flourish because of God's love: it never stops, cannot fail, and goes on forever and ever. Believers who trust that God's love never fails don't just survive—they thrive!

Have you ever had someone promise, "I'll never let you down"? Then, weeks or months later, they did fail you, maybe in a big way? Maybe you needed help on a school project, or comfort when you had your appendix out in the hospital. That "faithful friend" couldn't be found or be bothered. That really hurts.

People can be like that sometimes, but never God. His love and compassion and kindness and forgiveness never stop. *He* never lets you down.

If you trust in that love and his Word (leaning on it, relying on it) you can count on producing fruit and being successful. "He shall be like a tree planted by the rivers of water, that brings forth its fruit in its season, whose leaf also shall not wither; and whatever he does shall prosper" (Psalm 1:3 NKJV).

When a friend or family member lets you down—and they all will sometimes because they're human—turn to God instead. His love never fails. It's for a lifetime. Pray and ask for his love to fill your heart.

Be like "a tree planted by the rivers of water, that brings forth its fruit in its season" (Psalm 1:3 NKJV). Sink your roots down deep into God's unfailing love, look toward the Son, and flourish!

Did You Know

. . . that the dove Noah sent out while waiting for dry land to appear brought back an olive leaf? Olive trees must be very hardy to survive floods! (Genesis 8:11)

More To Explore: Psalm 92:12-15

Girl Talk:

Has anyone ever let you down? Have you let others down? Do you know God will never let you down?

God Talk:

"Lord, I know I'm not perfect, and neither is anybody else. Help me to lean on you. Thank you for never leaving me. Amen."

Fun Factoid:

Archeological evidence suggests that olives grew in Crete as long ago as 2,500 B.C. From Crete and Syria olives spread to Greece, Rome, and other parts of the Mediterranean area.

Devotion #66

"Pride goes before destruction, and a haughty spirit before a fall."—Proverbs 16:18 (NKJV)

Setting Yourself Up To Fall

It's good to think well of yourself—God does! But when your opinion of yourself is arrogant and you view yourself as superior to others, watch out! You're heading for a fall. You may only stumble, but you also may be totally destroyed.

Can you detect people with excessive pride? It's the girl who talks endlessly about her looks. It's the kid who says, "Everyone knows I'm the best soccer player on the team. If you work at it, maybe someday you'll be as good as I am." Sometimes pride is harder to spot. You congratulate someone on her science fair project, and she says, "Thank you. I worked hard on it." (She forgets to tell you that her friend did half the work.)

The hardest spot to detect pride is in your own heart. We look at someone's actions and think (or say), "*I'd* never do such a thing!" Be careful. Often when you think you're on solid ground, you're close to stumbling. "If you think you are standing strong, be careful, for you, too, may fall into the same sin" (1 Corinthians 10:12 NLT).

If you're tempted to be overly proud, take steps to correct that. "For through the grace given to me I say to everyone among you not to think more highly of himself than he ought to think" (Romans 12:3 NASB). When a prideful thought comes to you, remind yourself that everyone has talents and abilities, and you're no better (and no worse) than anyone else.

Deal strongly with pride. Your friends will thank you for it!

Did You Know

. . . that King Nebuchadnezzar, who ruled over the Israelites during the time of Daniel, lost his power and ate grass like a cow? See why in Daniel 4:28–37.

More To Explore: Proverbs 18:12 and Isaiah 2:11–12

GirL TaLk:

Have you ever said, "I'd never do such a thing"? And when you do something well, who do you give the credit to—you or God?

God TaLk:

"Lord, I know I sometimes think I'm better than others. Please help me to be humble and look only to you for praise. Amen."

Mini-Quiz:

Your teacher comments on how wonderful your science project is. You say:

A. Thanks so much. It is rather special.

B. Yes, it's really incredible, isn't it?

C. Thank you. My partner, Ashley, also worked hard on it.

Devotion #67

"But you desire honesty from the heart, so you can teach me to be wise in my inmost being."
—Psalm 51:6 (NLT)

GeT ReaL!

God wants you to be honest deep in your heart. Truth on the surface isn't enough. When you're honest in your innermost being, God can teach you to be wise and sensible in your speech and behavior.

Suppose the nicest (but least popular) girl in your class invites you to her birthday party. You squirm inwardly, but say, "I'd love to come." Then you search your brain for hours for an excuse to avoid going. If you go, you'll have a rotten time. If you lie to escape going, you'll feel guilty and she might find out.

Being honest with our lips is the first place to start. You could have said, "Thanks for asking me. I can let you know tomorrow." Total truth. You haven't lied, but you haven't committed yourself to anything yet. You don't have a touchy situation to deal with either.

But let's dig deeper, into your innermost being. God wants honesty from the heart. And the truth is that your heart has some dirty spots on it: pride, lack of love, fear of what others might think instead of what God thinks of your actions. This is the truth God wants you to face and 'fess up to. You may or may not choose to go to the party, but share with God what's really in your heart. Then he can teach you how to make the best decisions, to have wise speech and behavior with others.

Remember, God already knows your heart. So open up with him today—get real—and then get wise!

Did You Know

. . . Sophie and Fiona go through this same struggle, about what to say and how to say it, in *Sophie's World*?

More To Explore: Job 38:36

GirL TaLk:

Do you ever stretch the truth? In the past, when you haven't told the whole truth, how has it turned out?

God TaLk:

"Lord, sometimes I don't tell the truth. Help me to always speak truthfully and not make up things to impress others. Thank you. Amen."

Fun FacToid:

Mark Twain once said, "If you tell the truth, you do not have to remember anything." He is talking about the fact that if you tell a lie, you have to remember it in order to keep the story straight. Truth is always better, and it's easier to remember!

Devotion #68

"Let us then fearlessly and confidently and boldly draw near to the throne of grace . . . that we may receive mercy [for our failures] and find grace to help in good time for every need [appropriate help and well-timed help, coming just when we need it]."—Hebrews 4:16 (AMP)

Help Is On The Way!

As believers, we never have to be afraid to come to our Father, God. When we fail or do wrong things, we can be confident that he'll forgive us. When we have troubles, he gives generous help. God's help is suitable for the problem and comes just when we need it.

Is there a friend, parent or grandparent you run to for help? This person may not always listen to you and help you in just the right way. God is all-powerful and a hundred times more willing to help his children! And God is all-powerful. Your friend or parent may truly want to help you, but be unable to do anything. God knows exactly what to do for every situation and has the power to carry it out.

Sometimes your problems seem too small to bother God. Does he really want to hear about the fight with your friend? Yes! "Because of Christ and our faith in him, we can now come fearlessly into God's presence, assured of his glad welcome" (Ephesians 3:12 NLT).

Remember that God cares about every detail of your life. He cares about all your relationships, your hardships, and how you deal with temptation. Just ask! "So that we may boldly say, the Lord is my helper, and I will not fear what man shall do unto me" (Hebrews 13:6 KJV).

Whatever you need right now, why not go boldly to God? He's there, waiting to help you!

Did You Know

. . . that everyone who asks God for something will receive an answer? It may be the answer you want, or the better answer God wants for you. See Matthew 7:7–11.

More To Explore:
Ephesians 2:18–20 and Philippians 4:6–7

Girl Talk:

Do you ever want to ask God something, but feel it's not worth it? Who *do* you talk to?

God Talk:

"God, thank you for being there for me anytime I want to talk. Please help me remember that I can come to you about anything. I love you. Amen."

Devotion #69

"Give thanks to the Lord, for he is good; his love endures forever."—1 Chronicles 16:34 (NIV)

FiLL IT Up

Be grateful, and express your gratitude to the Lord, for he is good! His love and mercy will continue forever, from now through eternity. It never ends!

After you've run four times around the track during gym class, your fuel tank is low. You feel shaky, so you know you need an energy bar or drink. Inside, you also have a "love tank" that gets empty. God fills it whenever you spend time with him, reading his Word to just talking to him and letting him love you. And God is the only one who can fill that particular spot in your heart. But when it goes too long between God visits, your love tank gets close to empty. You won't get the shakes, but symptoms might include being impatient, rude, jealous, or just totally stressed. It means you're running on "empty" and need to refuel.

Good news! God's love is everlasting— it never runs out. Even better news—it's always available to us, just for the asking. It doesn't matter what time of the day or night it is. It doesn't matter where you are. It doesn't matter if you're alone or in a crowd.

When you realize that your love tank is getting low, stop. Get alone if you can, or just close your eyes. Take several deep, deep breaths. Then thank God for being such a good God and for his love, which never runs out. Ask him to "fill it up" while you wait in his presence.

God's love is everlasting, and the world is in desperate need of his love. Who can you share this good news with today?

Did You Know

. . . that Psalms 106:1, 107:1, 118:1, and 136:1 are all exactly the same? "Oh, give thanks to the LORD, for he is good! For his mercy endures forever" (NKJV). What a motto that is for you!

More To Explore: 2 Chronicles 5:13

Girl Talk:

Do you ever feel your "love tank" getting low? How do you usually fill yourself up again? Do you go to God?

God Talk:

"Thank you for your love, Lord. Please help me remember that you are with me always. Fill me up with your love every day. Thank you. Amen."

Fun Factoid:

In the NIV translation of the Bible, the word love is mentioned 710 times!

Devotion #70

"A wise man will hear and increase learning, and a man of understanding will attain wise counsel."
—Proverbs 1:5 (NKJV)

Anybody Listening?

A sensible, perceptive, and wise girl will listen and pay attention. By doing so, she'll acquire greater and deeper learning. A girl who wants the ability to make good judgments and decisions will search out sensible guidance and advice.

When you're excited to share something with your family or best friend, do you do all the talking? Do you "tune out" anything others might say because you're so focused on your own speech? Then you are missing an opportunity to grow and learn. When a teacher or parent tries to correct you about something, do you pay attention and consider what is said? Or are you content to simply appear as if you're listening, while you wait for them to finish and go away. Again, you've missed a chance to get smarter. Proverbs says you should do the opposite of tuning others out. You'd be much smarter, in fact, to seek out sensible people and ask for guidance.

Don't let your pride trick you into thinking you already know everything. Assume that you don't, and be open to learning from other (hopefully wiser) people in your life. Do two things. First, listen when others share their thoughts with you. Since you already know what YOU know, you won't learn anything by doing all the talking. Learning only increases when you *listen*. Second, if you have a decision to make ("Should I quit band?" "Should I go to that movie?"), seek out sensible, godly people and ask their advice.

Want to put yourself on the fast track to learning? Zip your lip, sharpen your ears, and become wise!

Did You Know

. . . that David was saved from doing something stupid due to wise advice from a woman? Read all about it in 1 Samuel 25:23–33.

More To Explore: Proverbs 9:9; 12:1

Girl Talk:

When you listen to others, are you really listening to them or thinking about what you will say next?

God Talk:

"Lord, thank you for always being a good listener. Help me to be a better listener. Thank you. Amen."

Beauty 101:

Pierced ears? If you have sensitive ears, buy nickel-free earrings. Don't pierce your upper ear (the cartilage above the lobe). It is easily infected, and the infections can damage the look of your ear forever!

Devotion #71

"Oh, how I love your law! I meditate on it all day long."—Psalm 119:97 (NIV)

Go Ahead—Soak It Up!

The psalmist, David, is talking about how much he loves God's Word, sometimes called "the book of the law" in the Old Testament. David loved God's Word so much that he reflected on it and thought about its meaning and observed how he could apply it. He meditated, soaking himself in God's Word.

Do you ever soak in a tub full of bubbles? It's soothing, peaceful, and totally relaxing—pure heaven. So is soaking in God's Word. When we love something, we love to think about it. You might love your new puppy or chocolate candy bars, so you think about them a lot. If you love a person, it's the natural thing to do to think about him. And if you love God's Word, his letters to us in the Bible, you'll spend time thinking about it. You'll ponder how to apply the words to your life.

When you soak in the tub, your skin wrinkles like a prune. That's changing from the outside in. When you soak in God's Word, he changes you from the inside out.

Meditating on scripture verses can replace stress with peace; sickness with healing; anger with compassion; hate with love; worry with faith; and weariness with energy. That's a lasting kind of make-over. If you have a special need right now— peace, rest, strength to persist—find a verse that specifically addresses that subject. Memorize it, or at least carry around the verse on a card. Then, at free moments during the day, read and think about the verse, especially how you could apply it to your life and situation.

Find a special verse right now. Copy it on a card then carefully think about it. Soak it up!

Did You Know

. . . that when memorizing something, there is a system to help you remember more effectively? Review what you have learned ten minutes after learning it, then a day, a week, a month after learning, and six months after learning. It will then be lodged in your long-term memory.

More To Explore: Deuteronomy 6:6–9 and Psalm 1:2

Girl Talk:

Use the Concordance at the back of your Bible or an online source to find a verse you want to memorize. Write it down, and read it several times today.

God Talk:

"Lord, thank you for giving me the Bible to answer my questions. Help me to look to your Word whenever I have a need. Amen."

Devotion #72

"And pray in the Spirit on all occasions with all kinds of prayers and requests."—Ephesians 6:18 (NIV)

Say a LiTTLe Prayer

Talk to God all the time. At every event, at every hour of the day, make all kinds of humble requests. Pray at critical times, but also pray when nothing special is happening. Take every chance and opportunity to talk to God, asking him for whatever you need or desire.

Pray on ALL occasions? When you're lonely? When you're at a party? When you wake up in the night? When you jog? When you eat? Yep—all those times, and more. God's interested in every detail of your life and loves you to share it with him. Don't you just love it when your best girlfriend calls to talk? You eagerly tell each other every tiny detail about your activities of the day. God feels the same way when we frequently take time out to talk to him.

Sometimes we don't pray much because we get too busy with things we need to do. We might only pray when we're in trouble or upset. We do pray more when in desperate need of guidance or comfort. But sometimes we don't pray because we don't know what to say. We are to "pray in the Spirit"—and it is the Holy Spirit who helps us to pray. "The Spirit helps us in our weakness. We do not know what we ought to pray for, but the Spirit himself intercedes for us with groans that words cannot express" (Romans 8:26 NIV).

Go ahead. Close this book and take a few minutes to tell God about your day. He's waiting to listen, and he's all ears.

Did You Know

. . . that supplication means earnest and humble prayer, even an act of begging? You will find a great example in Luke 18:1–7.

More To Explore:
Romans 12:12 NLT

Girl Talk:

How often do you pray to God? What do you tell him about?

God Talk:

"Lord, I'm glad I can talk to you whenever I need to. Thank you for always being available. Help me to remember to talk to you all the time. Amen."

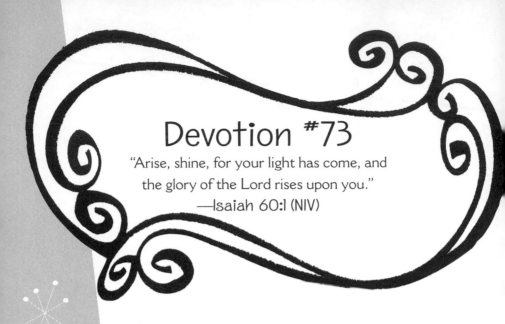

Devotion #73

"Arise, shine, for your light has come, and
the glory of the Lord rises upon you."
—Isaiah 60:1 (NIV)

WWJD?®

Get up and shine! Let the brilliant radiant beauty of
the Lord (who lives in you) come to the surface and make
you bright. As his child, you reflect his light. You should glow!
How can you reflect the love of Jesus in your life and to the
world around you? Have you seen the WWJD?® bumper
stickers, bracelets, and T-shirts? You probably know that it stands
for "What Would Jesus Do?" It's not just a clever slogan
though. It's supposed to be your way of life. Why? "For you
were once darkness, but now you are light in the Lord.
Walk as children of light" (Ephesians 5:8 NKJV).
You should stand out as different—in a
good way!

When you're in a situation where you
don't know what to do, stop and ask
yourself, "What would Jesus do?" By
choosing his actions, you'll reflect his
glory and your light will shine. What if a
new girl sits next to you in math, and she

smells bad? What do you do? Maybe you see a disabled woman trying to load groceries into the trunk of her car. What do you do? More importantly, what would *Jesus* do?

If you ask yourself this question throughout your day, you'll live and act differently than the rest of the world. Matthew 5:16 (NKJV) says, "Let your light so shine before men, that they may see your good works and glorify your Father in heaven."

Before you do or say something, stop and think, "What would Jesus do?" Then act accordingly—and just watch how you glitter and glow!

Did You Know

. . . that Jesus called himself the "light of the world"? Read John 8:12.

God Talk:

"Lord, help me to consider what you would do before I say or do anything. I want your light to shine bright in me. I love you Lord. Amen."

More To Explore: Philippians 2:15

Girl Talk:

Do you ever think about what Jesus would have done in different situations? Looking back at the past week, would Jesus be proud of your actions?

Devotion #74

"Don't let anyone look down on you because you are young, but set an example for the believers in speech, in life, in love, in faith and in purity."—I Timothy 4:12 (NIV)

Act Your Age!

Timothy was quite young when Paul wrote him this letter. People weren't taking Timothy seriously. Paul told him not to let anyone think less of him because he's young. Instead, Timothy guards his behavior and sets an example. He showed the believers how grown up he was by how he lived, how he loved people, his faith, and his sexual purity.

Adults watch the actions of some youths—their drinking, violence, foul language, and drugs—and, without thinking, judge all kids as being alike. Adults sometimes even look down on kids with scorn when observing some silly youthful behavior. Have any adults ever rolled their eyes at you and pleaded, "Act your age"?

Kids often complain that they're being treated like babies or small children. Here, Paul is giving you a guaranteed, sure-fire way to get the adults in your life to treat you with respect. If you set a good example of Christian conduct in what you say, in how you love and treat people, and in your spiritual walk and trusting God—you'll definitely get adult attention (the kind you want!). Age and maturity don't mean the same thing. Old people can be mature or very immature. Young people can be either one too. It's your choice. Whatever you choose, you will be known for your behavior and respected (or not) because of it.

Choose to be known for your faith, love, and purity. Then watch the adults in your life sit up and take notice!

Did You Know

. . . that Josiah became king of Judah when he was only eight years old? "He did what was right in the eyes of the Lord," and renewed the Covenant between the people and the Lord. See 2 Kings 22:1–23:30.

More To Explore:

1 Peter 5:3 and James 3:13

Girl Talk:

Do you ever feel passed over because you are young? Do you know that you can do as much for God as anybody else?

God Talk:

"Lord, I want to do great things for you. Help me to find out what you want me to do with my life. Thank you for your guidance. Amen."

Devotion #75

"The hand of the diligent will rule, but the lazy
man will be put to forced labor."
—Proverbs 12:24 (NKJV)

Diligence Rules!

Diligent people—those who persevere in carrying out
their jobs with care—are the people who will be the bosses.
So work hard and become a leader. Laziness will give you the
opposite result: forced labor! Want to be a leader or a slave?
The choice is yours.

The best paid babysitter who's always in demand is
diligent. She plays games with small children, she takes
First Aid classes, and she focuses on her task (instead of
the phone) while she's there. This babysitter will
"rule" the neighborhood and be able to charge
more per hour. At school, the person who
is best in spelling and grammar will get to
be the editor of your school paper. The
girl who takes extra voice lessons and
practices at home will get more solos.
Proverbs says diligent people will rule,
or be in charge. Are you diligent? When

you set a worthy goal (like reading one book per week, painting your bedroom, or mowing the lawn), do you continue until you're completely finished? Diligent people stay focused on their task and refuse to give up. They don't let problems or struggles make them quit. Eventually they have extra money, while people who rush through things have little. "The plans of the diligent lead surely to plenty, But those of everyone who is hasty, surely to poverty" (Proverbs 21:5 NKJV).

Be diligent, and don't settle for second best. Continue to strive to fulfill God's will for your life.

Did You Know

. . . that there are ways you can develop diligence with your school work, even if you have trouble concentrating? Learn how Faithgirlz! solve this kind of problem in *Sophie's World*.

More To Explore: Proverbs 13:4; 24:30–34

Girl Talk:

Do you finish tasks that you've started? How hard do you work at school, at jobs, at home?

God Talk:

"Lord, I want to be diligent in everything I do. Please help me to work hard and finish what I start. Thank you for being the perfect example. Amen."

Mini-Quiz:

Are you diligent? When your mom asks you to clean the bathroom, you:

(a) wipe off the countertop and call it good.

(b) scrub the toilet, tub, and sink even though it's gross.

Devotion #76

"Love is patient . . ."—I Corinthians 13:4 (NIV)

Patience Is a Virtue

Love in action endures difficult and trying events with a calm, even temper. A patient person handles difficult circumstances without protest or complaint. Displaying patience is especially hard when it comes to our families. It seems they know exactly which buttons to push. If you're in a hurry, your little brother will spill juice all over your new pants. If you're expecting a phone call from your best friend, your mom is sure to be on the phone with her office for hours. If you need help with your math homework, your father will have to work late. Bet on it.

We get a "patience test" every day. If you fail more often than not, if you snap at your brother or pout with your parents, trying harder won't necessarily do the trick. Patience is a fruit of the Spirit (Galatians 5:22). So the more you "hang out on the vine" with Jesus, the more fruit you'll grow—and that includes the fruit of patience. Your job isn't to try harder. Your job is to spend time with the Lord, reading his Word and praying.

Then be obedient to what the Holy Spirit prompts you to do. "But the ones that fell on the good ground are those who, having heard the word with a noble and good heart, keep it and bear fruit with patience" (Luke 8:15 NKJV).

How will you do on the test? When your brother spills on you, do you yell at him? Or do you listen to the quiet inner nudge that says, "Be kind. He didn't do it on purpose. Help him clean it up"? If you choose to be kind, your patience fruit will grow a little more.

God is love, and love is patient. How can you display the fruit of patience right now?

Did You Know

. . . that patience can also mean composure and self-control? That's staying cool under pressure.

More To Explore: Romans 15:5

Girl Talk:

When is it hard for you to be patient? Do you want to have more patience?

God Talk:

"Lord, thank you for your never-ending patience with me. Help me to be patient at all times, staying cool under pressure. Thank you for your love. Amen."

Fun Factoid:

One of our first presidents, John Quincy Adams, once said, "Patience and perseverance have a magical effect before which difficulties disappear and obstacles vanish."

Devotion #77

"A gentle answer turns away wrath, but a harsh word stirs up anger."—Proverbs 15:1 (NIV)

PuT OuT The Fire!

When someone is angry with you, you will make the fight worse if you answer with threatening or unkind words. On the other hand, a soft and gentle answer can put the fire out altogether.

Have you been spoken to harshly? We all have. Maybe your mom is angry with you, and she speaks sharply to you about the mess you and your friends left in the kitchen. Which answer is more likely to turn away your mom's anger? (1) "If you baked cookies like Sarah's mom, I wouldn't have to fix my friends a snack," or (2) "You're right. I shouldn't have left the mess. I'll clean it up right now"? Answer #1 could get you assigned kitchen duty for a week. Answer #2 might earn you a hug instead. Some moms would be so shocked by that response they'd help you clean up! Sometimes people get stirred up and say angry words when they want something badly. Maybe you want to go to a swim party, but your parents aren't satisfied about the lack of lifeguards planned. You really, really want to go. You plead, you cry, maybe you stomp your foot. Now they're angry and tell you to "watch yourself, young lady." A soft answer at this point will do a lot toward turning down the heated emotions. Then you can present your case calmly. "Patience can persuade a prince, and soft speech can crush strong opposition" (Proverbs 25:15 NLT).

When met with angry words today, pause and count to ten. Then smile, give a gentle answer, and watch that anger just melt away.

Did You Know

. . . that Solomon compared starting a quarrel to "breaching a dam," or breaking a hole into a dam? That can start a flood! See Proverbs 17:14 for Solomon's advice.

Girl Talk:

How do you respond when someone is angry with you? Do you think before you answer, or do you say something without thinking?

More To Explore: Proverbs 15:18

God Talk:

"Lord, sometimes I shoot off my mouth without thinking. Please help me to think before answering in anger. I want to be calm and collected, like you! Thank you. Amen."

Devotion #78

"Listening to gossip is like eating cheap candy.
Do you really want junk like that in your belly?"
—Proverbs 18:8 (MSG)

Junk Food Gossip

The words of a gossiping blabbermouth who spreads rumors are like junk food and cheap candy. It's very tempting, it tastes sweet, and looks harmless. But the gossip you listen to goes directly from your ears into your heart. It sinks deep, causing you pain and distress later.

Lots of restaurants, airports, and public buildings are smoke-free because studies show that breathing secondhand smoke was even more dangerous than smoking the cigarette yourself. If you breathe in someone else's cigarette smoke, you're getting it full-strength, unfiltered by the cigarette tip. The smoker's old excuse of "I'm not hurting anyone but myself by smoking" has proven totally false.

The same is true about listening to second-hand gossip, when someone tells you a private and juicy story about another person. Even if you hold your tongue and don't join in, and even if you don't repeat the gossip, you have still taken in second-hand poison. The rumors (whether true or false) will damage your opinion of the person talked about.

It's good that you don't repeat gossip, but take it one step further. Don't even listen to it. First, try changing the subject. If that doesn't work, stick up for the person being talked about. If the gossip-bearer still won't quit, walk away. Don't stand there and be a passive receiver of another girl's verbal poison.

Leave the cheap junk food candy behind, and become a health food nut. Your stomach—and your friends— will thank you.

Did You Know

. . . that a leader who gossips infects all his workers? Proverbs 29:12 says the workers are infected with evil!

More To Explore: Ephesians 5:4 and Proverbs 26:20–22

Girl Talk:

Have you found yourself enjoying gossip recently? What could you do next time when someone wants to share gossip with you?

God Talk:

"Lord, I know gossip is bad for me. Help me to remember not to listen to gossip and not to spread it. Thank you. Amen."

Beauty 101:

While you work on a healthy mind, make your diet healthier by eating more fish. Omega–3 acids in fish help boost your overall brain functioning. Try tuna, salmon, or herring.

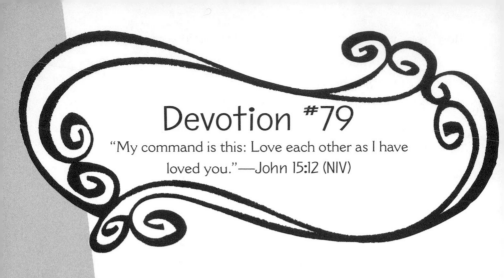

Devotion #79

"My command is this: Love each other as I have loved you."—John 15:12 (NIV)

Say I Love You a Million Ways

Jesus commands us to love each other. A command is an order, not just a nice-sounding suggestion. We are to love each other in the same way Jesus loved his disciples. God loves us by his words (the Bible) and by his actions, or the things he does in our lives and the blessings he showers on us. We are to love others in the same way: in words and in actions.

Is it hard for you to say "I love you"? It can be. With family members, getting mushy can be downright awkward and embarrassing if you're not used to it. With friends it can be considered "uncool" to say the words. But try saying them anyway: *I love you, I care about you, You mean a lot to me* . . . however you want to say it. Tell people how much you care about them—in spoken words, in little notes, in handmade cards—but tell them.

Don't stop there though. "Talk is cheap," as the saying goes. Words without similar actions are meaningless. If your friend says, "I really care about you," but she's always too busy to talk or listen to you, then her words will mean very little to you. If your grandmother says you're very important to her, but she always forgets your birthday and won't come to your school programs, then her words are hard to believe. So add actions to your words. Help your mom put away groceries. Help your dad with yard work. Pick some wildflowers for your sister's desk. Actions sometimes DO speak louder than words.

Be sure the people you love know it. Show them you love them, by your actions as well as your words, and do it today!

Did You Know

. . . that the commandment to love your neighbor as yourself is listed nine times in the Bible? God seems to think it's pretty important!

More To Explore: John 13:34–35 and I Peter 3:8

GirL TaLk:

How often do you tell your friends and family that you care about them? Do you ever tell God how much you love him?

God TaLk:

"Father, help me to show my family and friends that I love them. Teach me to love like you, Lord. Thank you. Amen."

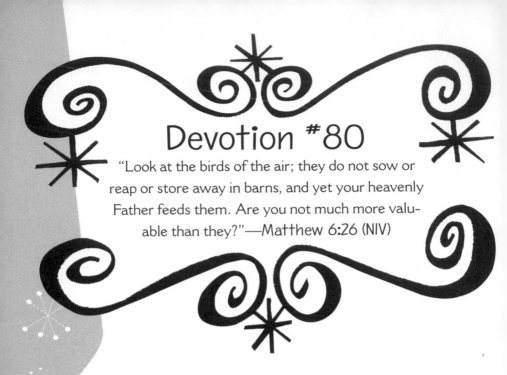

Devotion #80

"Look at the birds of the air; they do not sow or reap or store away in barns, and yet your heavenly Father feeds them. Are you not much more valuable than they?"—Matthew 6:26 (NIV)

The Master Bird Feeder

Instead of worrying about having enough food to eat, study the wild birds. They don't plant or harvest or put food in barns. They don't need to because God feeds them. You are much, much MORE valuable to God than the birds, so doesn't it make sense that he'll feed you and meet your needs too? Maybe you have plenty to eat. Your needs may be different. You may need a friend because you've just moved. You may need money for the school trip your class is taking to the water park. You may need help with your math problems. You may need help with your wild hair that has a mind of its own. Whatever your need, God has promised to meet it. "And this same God who takes care of me will supply all your needs from his glorious riches, which have been given to us in Christ Jesus" (Philippians 4:19 NLT).

God sees everything and knows what you need, even before you ask him. So don't be shy. Tell him what you need, and don't forget to thank him for his answers. "And do not seek what you should eat or what you should drink, nor have an anxious mind . . . your Father knows that you need these things . . . Do not fear, little flock, for it is your Father's good pleasure to give you the kingdom" (Luke 12:29–30, 32 NKJV).

See how carefree the birds are. As part of God's "little flock," you can be as free as a bird, without a worry, too. God will even more abundantly take care of YOU.

Did You Know

. . . that God brought food to the Israelites in the desert, where no food was available? God sent manna and quail every day for 40 years. He took care of the Israelites; he will take care of you! See Exodus 16.

Girl Talk:

Do you ask God for what you need? Do you know he will always take care of you?

More To Explore: Matthew 6:25–34 and Ephesians 3:16–19

God Talk:

"Lord, I am so thankful that you are always here with me. Please help me to rely on you for everything. Thank you. Amen."

Devotion #81

"Do not merely look out for your own personal interests, but also for the interests of others."
—Philippians 2:4 (NASB)

But What About Me?

Don't just think about your own needs and wants. Be interested in others and what they're doing. Look out for others as well as you look out for yourself.

Do you know people who only talk about themselves? When you eat a meal with them, the entire time they chatter on about *their* problems, *their* activities, *their* feelings, and *their* life. Even when you try to tell them something you've done, you're cut off or your words are ignored. They just want to talk about themselves. How much more fun is it to be with a girlfriend who also asks about your interests?

Besides being interested in other people and their lives, it's important to look out for them as well as yourself. In a crowded lunch room or school bus, don't just look for an empty seat for yourself; look for one for your friend as well. Instead of being "me-minded," train yourself to be "others-minded."

Romans 12:15 (NKJV) says that we should "rejoice with those who rejoice, and weep with those who weep." That means to set aside your own interests for a while. Is your friend thrilled about her A on the science test? Then be happy with her. Is she sad because her grandma died? Then be sensitive to that and tone down your stream of chatter. "But what about me?" you ask. You want "give and take" in your friendships. But you'll notice a wonderful thing that happens. While you're busy meeting a friend's need, God will meet yours.

Look out for others, and be interested in their lives. Be a true friend.

Did You Know

. . . that Sophie helps others in her class, especially Kitty, in *Sophie's World*? Sophie's not focused on herself, but on helping others.

More To Explore: I Corinthians 10:23–24 and Galatians 6:1–2

Girl Talk:

Do you tend to always talk about yourself? Do you focus on others' needs, not just your own?

God Talk:

"Lord, I want to listen to others better, and not just focus on myself. Please show me ways to help my friends and family. Thank you for being with me always. Amen."

Fun Factoid:

To help remind you that God should be your focus, wear a cross necklace, hang a small cross in your bedroom, or put a favorite verse in your diary.

Devotion #82

"He who despises his neighbor sins, but blessed is he who is kind to the needy."
—Proverbs 14:21 (NIV)

Howdy, Neighbor!

To despise your neighbor means to look down on someone with scorn and contempt—a total lack of respect mixed with intense dislike. Talk about a rotten attitude! On the other hand, a person is happy and blessed when he is kind to the poor and needy.

Your neighbors (at home or in school or church) might not look needy, but "poor" simply means "lacking" something, or not having enough. They might not have enough food. They could be lacking close friends or a good church home. Invite them to your home or church. You're doing it for them—but for God as well. "For I was hungry, and you fed me. I was thirsty, and you gave me a drink. I was a stranger, and you invited me into your home . . . 'I assure you, when you did it to one of the least of these my brothers and sisters, you were doing it to me!' " (Matthew 25:35–40 NLT).

Suppose someone new joins your Sunday school class. How can you be a good neighbor? You can help her find a place to belong, like youth group. Send her a card if she misses a few Sundays at church, just to let her know you're thinking about her. Introduce her to your other friends, and include her in your conversations. Create a "Welcome!" gift basket; include a map of the area, homemade cookies, and a personal note.

How can you be a good neighbor? Treat others the way you'd like them to treat you. You can't go wrong there!

Did You Know

. . . that the parable of the good Samaritan is a great story about being a good neighbor? Read Luke 10:25–37.

More To Explore: James 2:14–16 and 1 John 3:17

Girl Talk:

Do you know someone who could use a good neighbor? What can you do for them?

God Talk:

"Lord, I want to be a helpful, kind neighbor. Help me to reach out to those around me and show them your love. Amen."

Fun Factoid:

Two of the Ten Commandments deal with the relationship between you and your neighbor. Exodus 20:16–17 tells us that we should not give false testimony against our neighbor, and that we should not be envious of what our neighbor has.

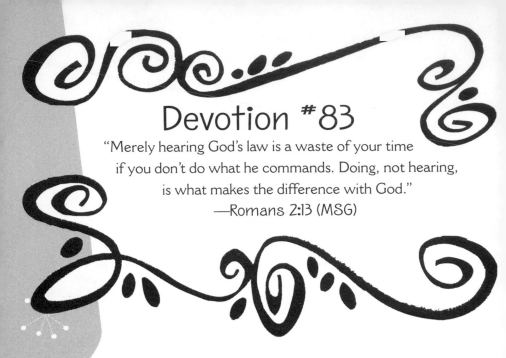

Devotion #83

"Merely hearing God's law is a waste of your time if you don't do what he commands. Doing, not hearing, is what makes the difference with God."
—Romans 2:13 (MSG)

Are You ALL <u>Talk</u> and No <u>Do</u>?

Unless you plan to do what the Bible says, just reading it is wasting your time. Being obedient—doing, not just hearing—is what God approves.

Maybe you know a girl in Sunday school who listens attentively. Yet at school, she acts stuck-up, tells dirty jokes and behaves totally different. What's going on? According to Romans, she's wasting her time at church because the words are going in one ear and out the other. Unless it changes your attitudes and behavior—unless you actually DO what the Bible says—your church attendance won't make any difference to God.

Are you that person yourself? Maybe you're not phony. Maybe you fully intend to do what God's Word says, like forgiving that person who gossiped about you, or being patient with your little brother. You haven't done it *yet* because it's too hard or you don't have time. Surely God will give you credit for good intentions, won't he? Sorry, but no. You won't be blessed by God simply for meaning to do something. The rewards are for the obedient, the ones who go beyond making promises and actually DO what the Father asks.

Be careful that you aren't proud of all your Bible knowledge, but then fail to put it into practice. So what if you can recite whole books of the Bible from memory, if you don't obey any of it? God would prefer that you know only three verses, if you actually put them into practice.

Be a doer of the Word, and not a hearer only.

Did You Know

. . . that the parable of two sons is a great example of actually doing something, not just talking about it? Read Matthew 21:28–31 for the story.

God Talk:

"Lord, I know I don't always do what I say I do. Please help me to do what you want me to do, not just read about it. Thank you that you are always encouraging me. Amen."

More To Explore:
Matthew 7:21 and James 1:22

Girl Talk:

Do you know what God's Word says, but aren't following it? How hard do you try to put God's Word into practice?

Devotion #84

"Love (God's love in us) . . . is not touchy or fretful or resentful."—1 Corinthians 13:5 (AMP)

Touchy, Touchy

If you're allowing God's love to flow through you and control you, then you won't be touchy with people. You won't be irritable, quick to take offense, and looking for trouble. A girl whose words and actions are controlled by God's love "doesn't fly off the handle" (MSG).

It's hard to be around touchy people. If you bump her on the bus, she turns and snarls at you. If you accidentally wear identical outfits to school, she says, "Thanks a whole lot!" and won't speak to you the rest of the day. If you don't move fast enough in the lunch line, she'll give you a shove from behind. Touchy people are tiring because, when you're around them, you have to keep your guard up. You never know when they're going to blow up.

Are you touchy? Pray for help. Ask God to change you on the inside so you're not so easily offended. He'll help you overcome this bad habit because, believe it or not, being touchy is a bad habit. It's a choice. And you can choose to lighten up, back off, count to ten, and shrug things off instead. If you tend to be thin-skinned, toughen up. "But that's just the way I am!" a girl cries. It's true that some girls are more irritable than others, but if that's you, get over it. Sometimes, you might have a *reason* to feel overly touchy, but don't let it become an *excuse* to stay that way.

When God's love flows through you to others, you won't be touchy. Most of the time you'll be good-natured and warm, friendly, and in good humor. Don't you just love being around people like that?

Did You Know

. . . that a righteous (blameless) tongue is compared to pure silver? Read more in Proverbs 10:20.

More To Explore:
Proverbs 14:17 and James 1:19-20

Girl Talk:

Do you ever act like a touchy person? What can you say instead when someone or something aggravates you?

God Talk:

"Lord, I know I can be touchy sometimes, and I don't want to be. Please help me to stay calm and be more loving. Thank you for your perfect example. Amen."

Beauty 101:

Some days can be touchier than others. Too much caffeine, hormones going crazy, too little sleep, not eating well, or a stressful time in your life can all produce touchy times. Keep an extra close watch on your mouth on these days!

Devotion #85

"Blessed are the peacemakers: for they shall be called the children of God."—Matthew 5:9 (KJV)

I Just Want Some Peace!

When others quarrel and fight, you will remain happy if you choose to be a peacemaker. Show people how to cooperate and work together instead of compete and argue. If you do this, you will understand your place in God's family.

When you quarrel with your sister or brother, does your dad ever mutter, "Can't we have some peace around here?" No one likes being around those who keep things stirred up and in turmoil. Have you ever been caught in the crossfire between bickering friends? Each girl wants you to take her side. Instead, be a peacemaker, and urge them to work together instead of fight. Help each one to understand the other's viewpoint. Even if those girls don't ever get along, you will be happier in the role of peacemaker. Refuse to be pulled into an argument. As much as it's up to you, get along with everyone. Unfortunately not everyone you meet *will* want to get along, but do your part. "If it is possible, as much as depends on you, live peaceably with all men" (Rom 12:18 NKJV).

That's a tall order, considering how unpleasant some people can be. Where can you find the power to do this? From Jesus himself. He said, "I am leaving you with a gift—peace of mind and heart" (John 14:27 NLT).

The more time you spend in God's Word and talking things over with him, the more peace you'll have to share, since peace is a fruit of the Spirit (Galatians 5:22).

Peacemakers are happy and content. They love to stay peaceful and to restore peace when it's broken. No matter what happens today, be determined to be a peacemaker.

Did You Know

. . . that Solomon was a peacemaker? He used his wisdom to help solve an argument between two women. Read the story in 1 Kings 3:16–28.

More To Explore:

Ephesians 4:1–3 and Hebrews 12:14

Girl Talk:

Do you ever find yourself caught in the middle of an argument? Do you tend to take a side or try to help them end the fight?

God Talk:

"Lord, it's hard to stay peaceful all the time. Please help me to stay out of arguments and work toward peace.

Thank you for being with me always. Amen."

Devotion #86

"So they cause the poor to cry out, catching God's attention. Yes, he hears the cries of the needy."
—Job 34:28–29 (NLT)

Grow a Bigger Heart

When the poor cry out for help, they catch God's attention. He hears the cries of those troubled by disease. He listens to those who have few material possessions.

Do *you* pay attention to the needs of the poor? You've seen Salvation Army bell ringers outside the stores, collecting money for the poor at Christmas time. Dropping some money in their red buckets is one way you could help. Don't promise to do it "the next time." Instead, donate your money right then, while you're there. "If you can help your neighbor now, don't say, 'Come back tomorrow, and then I'll help you'" (Proverbs 3:28 NLT).

Our country heard the cry of the needy, and many came here looking for a better life. The poem on the Statue of Liberty, written by Emma Lazarus in 1903, says it well: "Give me your tired, your poor, your huddled masses yearning to breathe free. The wretched refuse of your teeming shore. Send these, the homeless, tempest-tossed to me. I lift my lamp beside the golden door."

There are many ways you can reach out and help those in need. Ask your family to go with you to a local soup kitchen to serve food and share God's love with the poor. Clean out your closet for toys you've outgrown, clean them up, and donate them to a charity. Have a garage sale to earn money selling things you no longer use; then donate that money to a group who helps the poor.

Today, thank God for your many blessings, and be generous to share them with others.

Did You Know

. . . that the Salvation Army began as the Christian Mission? Started in 1865, its mission was to help, and hopefully convert, the people in the poorest part of London.

More To Explore: Proverbs 14:31

Girl Talk:

Have you ever helped someone less well-off than you? If so, how did that make you feel?

God Talk:

"Lord, I know there are many people who have so much less than I do. Please show me ways to help them and encourage them. I want to show them your love. Thank you. Amen."

Devotion #87

"How do you know what will happen tomorrow? For your life is like the morning fog—it's here a little while, then it's gone."—James 4:14-15 (NLT)

I'LL Do IT Tomorrow

Morning fog doesn't last long. It can be thick, but when the sun pops over the horizon, the fog is gone in a moment. Vanished like steamy vapor, without a trace. Our lives are brief like that. We don't know what will happen in the future—or even if we'll be around tomorrow.

Life is short, and you need to make the most of every day. Do you put things off like finishing book reports or washing laundry, saying, "I'll do that tomorrow"? (That's called "procrastination.") When tomorrow comes, do you put it off again? To be honest, we often have no intention of tackling that task tomorrow either. We just say that because it makes us feel better—for the moment anyway. Why do we do it? Laziness. Fear of failing. Too busy. Too tired.

Eventually you will bear the consequences of procrastinating. You may flunk the test you put off studying for. You won't have the clean leotard you need for tryouts because it's still buried in a pile of dirty clothes. You may also miss cool opportunities that God wanted you to have in the future. Perhaps an A on that writing project would have qualified you to win a state competition. But because of your procrastination, you weren't prepared, so the opportunity went to someone else.

Since life is short, the best time to get something done is *today*. It will brighten all your tomorrows and make them easier.

Did You Know

. . . that procrastination is associated with higher stress and poor health? Don't put things off! Your body will thank you.

More To Explore: Psalm 39:5

Girl Talk:

Do you ever put off something that needs to get done? How do you feel? What usually happens?

God Talk:

"Lord, I know I put things off sometimes. Help me to get things done on time, so that your plan for me is not interrupted. Thank you for caring so much. Amen."

5 Steps To Getting Productive!

1. Convince yourself: "The sooner I get this done, the sooner I can play."
2. Encourage yourself: "I can do all things through Christ who strengthens me."
3. Organize yourself: Keep a list of weekly goals visible, and check them off when done.
4. Prioritize yourself: List important things first, and do them first.
5. Reward yourself: Celebrate completing your tasks!

Devotion #88

"Good people are guided by their honesty;
treacherous people are destroyed by
their dishonesty."—Proverbs 11:3 (NLT)

Let Honesty Be Your Guide

Good people let honesty determine their course of action. Crooked people are defeated by their lying, cheating, and stealing.

Fibbing about why you were late, cheating "just a little" on a test, "borrowing" your friend's CD without asking—they're all forms of dishonesty. In the end, actions like these can destroy a life because dishonesty breeds even more serious dishonesty. On the other hand, if you want your life to be stable and successful, let honesty determine your course of action. Tell the truth about why you were late—even if you'll suffer consequences. Study for the test, then do the best you can without peeking at anyone else's paper.

Honesty will protect you. Doing what's right will shield you from danger and harm that results from an unholy lifestyle. Dishonesty—in all its forms—

causes the downfall of many people and destroys the life God meant for them to have. "Righteousness guards the one whose way is blameless, but wickedness subverts the sinner" (Proverbs 13:6 NASB).

Besides being honest with others, be honest with yourself. Examine your actions and the reasons behind them. For example, when you gave the new girl your cake at lunch, did you do it so she'd feel welcome in her new school? Or maybe you feel rejected at school, and you're secretly hoping to buy her friendship. Be honest with yourself and with God. Sometimes the truth hurts for a while, but it can make us free and help us grow.

Did You Know

. . . we are to be like a seed that falls on good soil? Luke 8:15 says that if we hear the word with an honest and good heart, we should hold it fast, and bear fruit with perseverance.

More To Explore: Proverbs 11:5

Girl Talk:

Are you honest with yourself? With others? Did you know that honesty can protect you?

God Talk:

"Lord, I know I am not always honest. Help me to be honest with myself and with others, especially you. Thank you for never giving up on me. Amen."

Devotion #89

"God is our refuge and strength, a tested help in times of trouble. Therefore we will not fear."
—Psalm 46:1-2 (NIV)

Safety in The Storms

When problems hit, we run to God. He is our safe place, our shelter from dangers and hardships. He's the source of our physical and mental toughness, endurance, and energy. God is a tried-and-true help in times of distress, problems, and pain. Because of that, we have nothing to fear. If you fall into the deep end of the pool, but can't swim, a lifeguard will rescue you. Usually we need rescuing from things less obvious than drowning. You might have two papers to type, and your computer breaks. Or perhaps you agreed to be the hostess for your class barbecue, but now it's raining, and you have no place to put fifty classmates. Help! Maybe someone stole your wallet and bus ticket, and you're stranded downtown without a way to get home. Or, more seriously, maybe you or someone you know is being abused at home. In all these cases, someone must come to your rescue. It's OK to ask a trusted adult for help—especially if someone is being abused.

How do we make God our shelter from storms and the strength we need to get through these situations? By prayer and faith. Sometimes the rescue comes immediately. Other times it takes a while. Sometimes the answer from God is to take action. Other times the answer is to keep reading your Bible. But the help WILL come. God has promised it. Stand firm until the answer comes, and "imitate those who through faith and patience inherit the promises" (Hebrews 6:12 NKJV).

Because of that assurance, take courage. Help is on the way!

Did You Know

. . . that the Lord is a strong tower? Proverbs 18:10 says that "the righteous run to it and are safe." Calling on God gives you a fortress of protection!

More To Explore: Psalm 62:7–8; Psalm 13:5

Girl Talk:

Have you ever asked God to rescue you? How did he answer you?

God Talk:

"Lord, I need your help every day. Thank you for always being here for me. I know I can always call on you. Amen."

Fun Factoid:

The word "rescue" occurs in the Bible 122 times. The word "save" is in the Bible 311 times. God is definitely in the business of rescuing and saving us!

Devotion #90

"Trust God from the bottom of your heart. Don't try to figure out everything on your own. Listen for God's voice in everything you do, everywhere you go. He's the one who will keep you on track."
—Proverbs 3:5–6 (MSG)

Your Constant Guide

Lean on God, and be confident in him. Let your heart rest in this trust. Don't depend on your own insight to figure things out. Instead, listen for the inner nudges from God throughout your day. Look to your Bible, do what he asks, and God will direct your steps. Be willing to ask for the advice of godly people. And trust your own God-given common sense.

If you hike through the wilderness in a national park, you can hire a guide. He'll keep you on safe paths, away from bears and poisonous snakes. He'll show you the clean streams for drinking water and lead you by the prettiest scenery. Or you can go out on your own. Your chances of snake bite, bear attack, polluted water, and falling off a cliff increase immediately.

Your life is like a path through that wilderness, and God is your committed guide. The hike may still be strenuous, but you'll have a safer and much more enjoyable experience. Coming up with your own plan and ignoring God and his Word can put you in the way of many dangers and unnecessary tough times. Avoid being a know-it-all. "Don't be impressed with your own wisdom. Instead, fear the LORD and turn your back on evil" (Proverbs 3:7 NLT).

Trust God and keep on a well-guided path that will lead to inner beauty and outward faith.

Did You Know

. . . that God went before the Israelites in a pillar of cloud by day and a pillar of fire by night? After they left Egypt, God was their guide. See Exodus 13:17–22.

More To Explore: Psalm 37:3–6 and Proverbs 28:26

Girl Talk:

Do you ever feel lost? Do you ever strike out on your own, with no guidance? Have you ever asked God for help?

God Talk:

"Father, I know I go off on my own sometimes. Help me to trust in you and follow your will for my life. I love you, Lord. Amen."

faiThGirLz!

Faithgirlz!™–Inner Beauty, Outward Faith

Sophie's World (Book 1)
Written by Nancy Rue
Softcover 0-310-70756-0

Sophie's Secret (Book 2)
Written by Nancy Rue
Softcover 0-310-70757-9

Sophie and the Scoundrels (Book 3)
Written by Nancy Rue
Softcover 0-310-70758-7

Sophie's Irish Showdown (Book 4)
Written by Nancy Rue
Softcover 0-310-70759-5

Available now or coming soon to your local bookstore!

Zonderkidz.

faiThGirLz!
Faithgirlz!™–Inner Beauty, Outward Faith

Sophie's First Dance? (Book 5)
Written by Nancy Rue
Softcover 0-310-70760-9

Sophie's Stormy Summer (Book 6)
Written by Nancy Rue
Softcover 0-310-70761-7

Available Now!

No Boys Allowed Devotions for Girls
Written by Kristi Holl
Softcover 0-310-70718-8

Available now or coming soon to your local bookstore!

Zonderkidz.

faiThGirLz!™

Also from Inspirio

inspirio

The gift group of Zondervan

Faithgirlz!™ Frame
ISBN: 0-310-80714-X

Faithgirlz!™ Cross
ISBN: 0-310-80715-8

Faithgirlz!™ Journal
ISBN: 0-310-80713-1

Available now or coming soon to your local bookstore!

Get FREE stuff when you purchase Faithgirlz!™ products!
Find out how easy it is …
Visit **faithgirlz.com** for details—
it's the place for girls ages 8–12!!

Zonder**kidz**®

We want to hear from you. Please send your comments about this
book to us in care of zreview@zondervan.com. Thank you.

Zonder**kidz**.

Grand Rapids, MI 49530
www.zonderkidz.com